Praise for

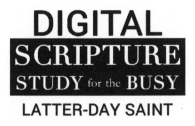

DIGITAL SCRIPTURE STUDY for the BUSY LATTER-DAY SAINT

"Truly studying the scriptures has become increasingly difficult because of the many modern distractions we experience today. Richard Bernard has given us a simple but comprehensive guide for getting back into and feasting upon the scriptures. I highly recommend this book!"

—GREG TRIMBLE, author of *The Missionary Special Forces* and *Dads Who Stay and Fight* and founder of Yalla and Lemonade Stand

"In 1974, President Spencer W. Kimball said, 'I believe that the Lord is anxious to put into our hands inventions of which we laymen have hardly had a glimpse.' If anything qualifies as an invention to be put into 'our hands,' it is the smartphone with all of its attendant capabilities. Brother Bernard has increased my capability and efficiency in gospel digital fluidity, which has sharpened my study and enhanced the breadth and depth of my ministry. Because of Seven Minutes, I am a better instrument for my family, congregation, and associates both in and out of the Church. In the same talk, President Kimball had this to say about our digital capability: 'Then, and not until then, shall we approach the insistence of our Lord and Master to go into all the world and preach the gospel to every creature.' The concepts, advice, and direction given in the highly accessible *Digital Scripture Study for the Busy Latter-day Saint* is certainly a strong move in getting us to the endline."

—DAVID GRANT, COO of the More Good Foundation

"The Gospel Library is an incredible tool that has added to my studying and enjoyment of the scriptures. Being able to include my thoughts, other scripture, various articles, and other links in an organized matter has enhanced my faith and immensely improved my scholarly studying of the scriptures. I recommend this book to anyone who wishes to further their study skills and become more well versed in the gospel."

—GREGORY NIELSEN, MD

"I have used the Gospel Library app for years—basically for highlighting and adding a few notes, but after taking [Richard's] class, I'm using it so much more! Now I can find scriptures *quickly*, open multiple screens to be used simultaneously, create my own topical files with the tagging system, link scriptures together, link quotes or articles to scriptures, add very detailed notes anywhere, copy and paste quickly, bookmark several different books and keep track of the page I'm on, create entire files on any subject in great detail (and these files are searchable when I want to find it again)—and all with the ability to 'share' at the touch of a button.

"Understanding these functions has made my scripture study so much more effective and enjoyable. I can still use my hard copy and take notes in the app, and I always have my notes with me. It has given me an organized way of documenting any information (not just religious) with the ability to retrieve it as needed. Thank you so much!"

—Karie Chaney

"The information I received from Richard Bernard's tutorial on using the Gospel Library has blessed my life. I use the tips and tricks daily in my personal gospel study and have shared liberally with those within my sphere of influence. I have presented Richard's information formally to stake presidencies, high councils, bishoprics, seminary and institute directors, and youth classes. In every exchange, there was insight gained and skills improved to making using the Gospel Library more effective with an immediate enhancement to gospel study."

—Patricia DuBray

DIGITAL
SCRIPTURE
STUDY for the BUSY
LATTER-DAY SAINT

DIGITAL
SCRIPTURE
STUDY for the BUSY
LATTER-DAY SAINT

7
MINUTES
A
DAY

RICHARD BERNARD

CFI
An imprint of Cedar Fort, Inc.
Springville, Utah

ISBN 13: 978-1-4621-2304-9

Published by CFI, an imprint of Cedar Fort, Inc.
2373 W. 700 S., Springville, UT 84663
Distributed by Cedar Fort, Inc., www.cedarfort.com

LIBRARY OF CONGRESS CATALOGING-IN-PUBLICATION DATA

Names: Bernard, Richard, 1948- author.
Title: Digital scripture study for the busy Mormon : 7 minutes a day /
    Richard Bernard.
Description: Springville, Utah : CFI, an imprint of Cedar Fort, Inc., [2018]
    | Includes bibliographical references and index.
Identifiers: LCCN 2018042756 (print) | LCCN 2018047412 (ebook) | ISBN
    9781462129539 (epub, pdf, mobi) | ISBN 9781462123049 (perfect bound : alk.
    paper)
Subjects: LCSH: Church of Jesus Christ of Latter-day Saints--Sacred
    books--Study and teaching. | Mormon Church--Sacred books--Study and
    teaching. | Electronic books--Handbooks, manuals, etc. | LCGFT: Handbooks
    and manuals.
Classification: LCC BX8622 (ebook) | LCC BX8622 .B47 2018 (print) | DDC
    289.3/2--dc23
LC record available at https://lccn.loc.gov/2018042756

Cover design by Wes Wheeler
Cover design © 2019 Cedar Fort, Inc.
Edited by Valene Wood and Allie Bowen
Typeset by Kaitlin Barwick

Printed in the United States of America

10 9 8 7 6 5 4 3 2 1

Printed on acid-free paper

Wherefore, I said unto you, feast upon the words of Christ; for behold, the words of Christ will tell you all things what ye should do.

2 NEPHI 32:3

Net proceeds will be donated to the general missionary fund.

CONTENTS

ACKNOWLEDGMENTS

As with the publication of any book, it cannot come to fruition without the support and encouragement of others.

First, a big thank you to Tracy Daley of Cedar Fort Publishing. Her belief in this book was unbelievable, and her input about the format of this book was invaluable. To Kaitlin Barwick for her input and keeping things on schedule. Also, thank you to all of the staff at Cedar Fort for their hard work and input.

A special thanks to the hundreds of missionaries I had the privilege of working with one-on-one in helping them with their scripture-study skills. Little did they know that I learned far more from them than they learned from me. Much of what is in this book is there because of my experience with these humble servants of the Lord.

There is another group that was also instrumental in the formation of this book: the senior missionaries from the Orem and Provo missions who attend the weekly Senior Missionary Geeks class I teach at the More Good Foundation. I am grateful for their patience and wonderful examples as they helped me to formulate various ideas that are in this book. Each week I am honored to be in their presence.

A thank you to all those, who are far too numerous to mention, who gave their honest feedback and encouragement.

I am also grateful to the two women who have greatly impacted my life and made this book possible. First, my wife of thirty-eight years, Claudia, who after a ten-year battle with cancer finally was taken from us. It was she that discovered that I had dyslexia and, with her patience and excellent command of languages, helped me—over nearly a twenty-year period—learn to write a coherent sentence. Without her help in learning to write, this book would never have been attempted.

To my wife of twelve years, Amy. She is my biggest supporter and believes in me even when I find it hard to believe in myself. She is my light each morning and my comfort at night; she makes each day a delight and creates an atmosphere at home that encourages not only my writing but any other endeavors I pursue. Because of her I want to be a better man than what I am.

PREFACE

Do you feel overwhelmed? Too much to do and not enough time to do it? Falling into bed at night exhausted and feeling guilty about the things you did not get done? Work. Children. Husband. Wife. Soccer. Errands. Church.

Church?

Yes, you know! Those things buried deep within your brain, the area where all your guilt resides. Guilt about temple attendance or lack thereof. Guilt over the collection of family history that gathers more dust each week. Guilt because you're trying to attend to your calling but you feel like you never do enough. Guilt thinking of the service for others that goes undone, family home evenings that feel rushed or unsatisfying, family prayers that are an exercise in the fight of wills, personal prayers that are short on words and done while driving to work or taking the children to more places than you care to mention. What about scripture study? Can't remember the last time you read the scriptures, let alone seriously studied them? Yes, we have plenty to feel guilty about. After all, doesn't the Savior tell us, "Be ye therefore perfect, even as your Father which is in heaven is perfect" (Matthew 5:48)?

It is time to take a deep breath.

The problem is that we tend to take those words from Matthew 5 literally. Elder Holland in the October 2017 general conference talked about perfection and that we will be perfected—eventually.[1] We need to be reminded of the words of President Nelson, who said, "Perfection is pending. It can come in full only after the Resurrection and only through the Lord."[2]

Way too many of the members of the Church feel guilt because, from their perspective, they are not doing enough. And this is not a new problem. Elder Dean L. Larsen noted over thirty years ago, "I seem to be encountering more and more frequently in my circulation among the

---

1. Jeffrey R. Holland, "Be Ye Therefore Perfect—Eventually," *Ensign*, Oct. 2017.
2. Russell M. Nelson, "Perfection Pending," *Ensign*, Nov. 1995.

membership of the Church, people who are honestly trying to avoid sin, who are really doing their best, as they understand, to live in accordance with the principles of the gospel but who are unhappy, frustrated, and disillusioned to a considerable degree.[3]

We need to stop punishing ourselves and remember that the purpose of life is to have joy (2 Nephi 2:25). We simply need to do the best we can, and the Savior will take care of the rest. We need to make His Atonement effective in our lives.

One of the greatest aids we have in learning how to find comfort and direction is personal revelation, and personal revelation is best accessed through prayerfully studying the scriptures.

Personal revelation provides for us perspective, insight, and instructions, so we will be able to handle whatever life throws our way without feeling overwhelmed, frustrated, or guilty.

For example, when I read Doctrine and Covenants 4, I am overcome with emotion. Left with a feeling of total inadequacy. Overwhelmed with all that is being asked. And filled with guilt because I am not doing enough.

I feel that I might as well throw in the towel and walk away—until I read verse 7: "Ask, and ye shall receive; knock, and it shall be opened unto you."

In those thirteen words is the answer to how to accomplish all that has been outlined in the previous verses, and the answer is simple: ask, and the Lord will show the way through personal revelation.

This book is about two great principles, "line upon line, precept upon precept; here a little, and there a little" (D&C 128:21); and "that by small and simple things are great things brought to pass" (Alma 37:6).

Most likely you have, in your possession right now, a smartphone. It is a powerful device given to you by Heavenly Father to enable you to make the best use of your time in hastening His work.

During the next fourteen days, you will learn how to use this device and all the powerful tools contained in the Gospel Library. The application is available for Apple, Android, and Windows, which comprise over 90 percent of all smartphones. In addition, if you do not have a smartphone or tablet, the Gospel Library app is also available online, so you can use your desktop or laptop computer.

---

3. Dean L. Larsen, "My Peace I Give unto You," *AMCAP Journal,* 1986, 12–13.

The tools are easy to learn and are presented in a simple format. This book will help you learn how to apply these tools to what you are studying in easy seven-minute sessions.

Do not underestimate what a few small minutes can do. Marvelous things will occur as a result of those seven minutes. You will draw closer to the Savior and find an inner peace that will serve you throughout the day. Over time you will develop mental, emotional, and spiritual strength. Personal revelation will come, providing you with greater understanding of the gospel and personal direction on how to better manage your day. As a result, your study time will increase to fit your personal schedule.

The Lord has put these wonderful and powerful devices into your hands, along with the Gospel Library, to enable you, in these busy latter days, to hasten His work, engage in missionary work, strengthen your testimony, be converted unto Christ, and fortify yourself against the temptations of the day.

Elder Christoffel Golden Jr. said this about the Gospel Library: "The Church has dedicated significant effort to improve this app in order to support Church members as they seek to increase their gospel learning and inspiration using mobile devices. **We encourage members to use it to enhance their study and draw near to the Lord and His holy prophets.**"[4]

You have the tools in your hands—now can you spare just 7 minutes?

---

4. Christoffel Golden Jr., "Major Upgrade for Gospel Library App for iOS Devices Announced," *Church News*, Jun. 25, 2013; emphasis added.

HOW TO USE THIS BOOK

This book is divided into five sections.

- **Section One** builds a foundation for the other sections. Please take the time to read and ponder the information.
- **Section Two** helps you master the tools contained in the Gospel Library.
- **Section Three** contains examples on how to engage in serious scripture study using the tools presented in this book.
- **Section Four** shares ideas on how to use your devices in preparing lessons, engaging in missionary work, and other various related topics. It will help you gain true mastery over your device.
- **Section Five** contains helpful information for those who are unfamiliar with technology terms or struggle using mobile devices in general.

Each chapter in Section Two has a Novice section that can be completed in seven minutes. During that time, you will study some scripture and apply one tool from the Gospel Library.

Do not be consumed with completing something in seven minutes. Everyone has different skill levels and experiences. If it takes you longer than seven minutes, stop and resume the next day. Just remember to always start and end with prayer.

Follow the counsel King Benjamin shared with his people: "And see that all these things are *done in wisdom and order*; for it is *not requisite that a man should run faster than he has strength*, And again, it is expedient *that he should be diligent*, that thereby he might win the prize; therefore, all things must be done in order" (Mosiah 4:27; emphasis added).

Joseph Smith, after losing the 116 pages of manuscript, received similar counsel: "Do not run faster or labor more than you have strength and means provided" (D&C 10:4).

So do what you can and be persistent, and the blessings will come.

What is important is you understand how to use the tool while developing good study habits.

Remember that we learn best when we take here a little and there a little. Heavenly Father is not so concerned with your speed as He is with your direction.

So if it takes you longer than seven minutes, then bookmark where you stopped (see Day 15 on how to bookmark) and continue the next day.

Most of the chapters in Section Two are divided into three skill levels:

- **Novice**—those who need detailed step-by-step basic instruction
- **Intermediate**—those who feel fairly comfortable with their device and need less detailed instruction
- **Advanced**—those who need very little explanation and do well with the big picture

Not all sections have Intermediate and Advanced sections because some of the tools are simple to cover. For those who are at an intermediate or advanced skill level, you should be able to go through the lesson quickly without further explanation.

The Novice section is often followed by a Going Deeper section, which builds on the basic skill the novice just learned. It can be read immediately after finishing the Novice section, if time permits, or in the future.

SUGGESTIONS FOR THE NOVICE

Please read Section Five before learning about the tools in the Gospel Library.

The *Conventions and Terminology* chapter will provide you with definitions of terms used throughout the book and includes screenshots. Bookmark it so you can refer to it as needed.

The chapter on UI awareness will explain a basic principle that everyone who is comfortable using mobile devices has unknowingly developed. Learning this principle will be a great help to you in your daily use of your device in general and the Gospel Library specifically as you become principle-based in using your mobile device over the years.

Lastly, as you become more proficient in the use of the Gospel Library, read the Intermediate skill level in Section Two and then move on to the Advanced level after that.

THIS BOOK IS PRINCIPLE BASED

Since technology changes at a blinding speed, a book on using technology or a how-to book on using an application is temporary at best. As technology changes, so do the applications that operate within the confines of the technology. New options become available, and often the placement of the options within the application are moved, combined, or deleted.

In addition, the hardware will also change to take advantage of the advanced technology. For example, the smartphones we use today will likely be very different than what we will be using in five years.

The basic principles, however, will not change. For that reason, this book is based on principles, the first being UI awareness, which is discussed in full in Section Five. The second is understanding the purpose of an application. The options available in an application depend on the purpose of the application.

For example, the main options (or tools) available in a word-processing application are different than options used in a spreadsheet application.

The Gospel Library is a database. The purpose of a database is to organize, input, and retrieve information. Searching, creating notes, linking to other parts of the database, and other basic tools are expected functions in a database application.

For example, knowing that the Gospel Library is a database, I would expect to find a search function. Finding where that search function is requires UI awareness. Using the search function effectively requires experimentation.

If you use UI awareness and understand the purpose of the application, then you can use an application with a sense of what it can and cannot do. You are then able to interact with the application with greater ease and adapt as changes occur.

SCREENSHOTS

Because I am using principles, I have tried to keep the number of screenshots to a minimum.

I use more screenshots with the novice-level tutorials and try to wean novices away as they progress.

At times I will show a screenshot of an iPhone and not of an Android when what I am showing is basically the same on both devices. I use the iPhone because it is my phone of choice, and more important, my iPhone communicates easier with my Mac than my Android does in the creation of this book.

Yes, I am, without any embarrassment, a fan of Apple. (And yes, I have contributed greatly to help them amass their billions.)

However, for many years I used Android phones (and still use one today) and PCs. For personal reasons, I switched to Apple. I believe that iOS and Android have excellent phones and tablets. I understand both sides of the argument of which is better, and there is no winning either way. It all comes down to personal preference. So forgive me if I show a preference to Apple with the screenshots.

FOR MORE HELP

For answers to further questions and to find additional tips and videos, visit TheBusyLatterDaySaint.com.

SECTION ONE

Your Personal Urim and Thummim

Nephi said, "Wherefore, if ye shall press forward, feasting upon the word of Christ, and endure to the end, behold, thus saith the Father: Ye shall have eternal life" (2 Nephi 31:20). What a tremendous promise.

The word "feast" comes from the Latin word *fester*, meaning "to celebrate." The Spanish word *fiesta* comes from this root. It is related to the word *fanum*, which means "temple," also meaning "to take pleasure or delight in something." Figuratively it means "to dwell with gratification or delight; not to take lightly but to indulge."

Not only are we to feast upon the scriptures, but we are also to drink deeply from them. Elder Bednar said, "The scriptures contain the words of Christ and are a reservoir of living water to which we have ready access and from which we can drink deeply and long. You and I must look to and come unto Christ, who is 'the fountain of living waters' (1 Nephi 11:25; Ether 8:26, 12:28), by reading (Mosiah 1:5), studying (D&C 26:1), searching (John 5:39; Alma 17:2), and feasting (2 Nephi 32:3) upon the words of Christ as contained in the holy scriptures. By so doing, we can receive both spiritual direction and protection during our mortal journey."[5]

Clearly the scriptures should not be treated casually; they are not mere words on a page. The scriptures provide us with direction and protection during our earthly lives.

---

5. David A Bednar, "A Reservoir of Living Water," (Brigham Young University devotional, Feb. 4, 2007), speeches.byu.edu.

President Ezra Taft Benson said in the April 1986 general conference, "[The Lord's] will is made manifest through the standard works, His anointed servants, and personal revelation."[6]

The scriptures not only contain revelation given to prophets for our benefit but also provide us with personal revelation. Elder D. Todd Christofferson stated, "Scriptures are revelation, and they will bring added revelation."[7]

President Dallin H. Oaks expressed the same sentiment: "Scripture is not limited to what it meant when it was written but may also include what that scripture means to a reader today."

President Oaks further remarked, "We do not overstate the point when we say that the scriptures can be a Urim and Thummim to assist each of us to receive personal revelation."[8]

While reading the scriptures is beneficial, studying them is far more beneficial. Studying leads to understanding. St. Hilary of Poitiers, bishop of Poitiers, France, in the fourth century, said, "Scripture consists not in what one reads, but in what one understands."[9] It is in that process of understanding that revelation can come.

While scripture appears simple in form, it is a means of receiving insight, guidance, and personal revelation; it is "a lamp unto [our] feet, and a light unto [our] path" (Psalm 119:105). Scriptures quench "the fiery darts of the adversary" (1 Nephi 15:24) and provide a way for us to take upon His name more fully, to become even as He is.

Elder Richard G. Scott said, "Scriptures are like packets of light that illuminate our minds and give place to guidance and inspiration from on high. They can become the key to open the channel to communion with our Father in Heaven and His Beloved Son, Jesus Christ."[10]

President Oaks encouraged us "to make careful study of the scriptures and of the prophetic teachings concerning them and to prayerfully seek personal revelation to know their meaning for themselves.[10]

Elder Bruce R. McConkie said, "May I suggest, based on upon personal experience, that faith comes and revelations are received as a direct result of scripture study."

6. Ezra Taft Benson, "A Sacred Responsibility," *Ensign*, May 1986.

7. D. Todd Christofferson, "The Blessing of Scripture," *Ensign*, May 2010.

8. Dallin H. Oaks, "Scripture Reading and Revelation," Ensign, Jan. 1995.

9. Hilary, *Ad Constantium Augustum* II, 9, in *PL* 10:570.

10. Richard G. Scott, "The Power of Scripture," *Ensign*, Nov. 2011.

He continues, "Paul says, 'faith cometh by hearing' the word of God. Joseph Smith taught that to gain faith men must have a knowledge of the nature and kind of being God is; they must have a correct idea of his character, perfections, and attributes; and they must so live as to gain the assurance that their conduct is in harmony with the divine will. Faith is thus born of scriptural study. Those who study, ponder, and pray about the scriptures, seeking to understand their deep and hidden meanings, receive from time to time great outpourings of light and knowledge from the Holy Spirit."[11]

Elder David A. Bednar expressed the same thought when speaking to students at a Ricks College devotional. He said, "Scripture study is a preparation for and prerequisite to receiving personal revelation."[12] It is clear how dear our leaders hold the scriptures and personal revelation.

As stated in the beginning, the scriptures are there for us to feast upon and to drink deeply from. Through that process, we are privileged to receive revelation as needed.

As stated earlier in this chapter, Elder Oaks refers to the scriptures as a Urim and Thummim. I like that analogy. The Bible Dictionary states that *Urim and Thummim* is a "Hebrew term that means 'Lights and Perfections.' An instrument prepared of God to assist man in obtaining revelation from the Lord."

The Urim and Thummim compares well with the Gospel Library because the Gospel Library is more than scripture; it is a vast library of material to help us in our study of the scriptures, and through studying comes light that will lead us to perfection. Like the Urim and Thummim, the Gospel Library is a gift from Heavenly Father.

A LAMP UNTO YOUR FEET

The scriptures are one of the keys to revelation, but how do we know we are receiving revelation? Often the mention of revelation brings up images of angels, prophets of old, or even the Savior appearing before us, but such is a rarity, as is hearing a voice from the heavens.

---

11.   Bruce R. McConkie, *"Holy Writ Published Anew,"* Regional Representatives Seminar, Apr. 2, 1982.

12.   David A. Bednar, "Understanding the Importance of Scripture Study" (Ricks College devotional, Jan. 6, 1998), http://www2.byui.edu/Presentations/Transcripts/Devotionals/1998_01_06_Bednar.htm.

We experience revelation usually in one of two ways; through the mind or feelings.

Enos said, "Behold, the voice of the Lord came into my mind" (Enos 1:10). In regard to Enos's quote, Boyd K. Packer remarked, "While this spiritual communication comes into the mind, it comes more as a feeling, an impression, than simply as a thought. Unless you have experienced it, it is very difficult to describe that delicate process."[13]

My personal experience has shown me again and again the truth of which Elder Packer speaks. I have learned the importance that praying and studying and pondering the scriptures plays in receiving personal revelation. While I do not expect revelation each time I study, it comes often enough and always at the right time. It guides me in the right direction, enlightens my mind, and helps me understand His works a little better and my role and responsibilities within them. I have seen the same happen to others.

I had the honor of serving a two-year service mission at the Provo Missionary Training Center. My responsibilities varied, but by far the greatest honor I had was working with missionaries who were struggling with studying the scriptures. I would meet with an elder or sister several times one-on-one and teach him or her how to study the scriptures.

Many times, when it was time to part ways, they would thank me for all that they learned. Little did they realize that I was equally the student and learned just as much from them. To be in their presence was indeed an honor, and each time I left them I thanked Heavenly Father for the privilege of being with them.

The last lesson I would teach them was about comprehending the scriptures. I'd like to share with you two experiences from teaching this lesson that exemplify the power and means of personal revelation as a result of studying the scriptures.

I sat with a sweet and humble sister one afternoon as we read and studied Mosiah 17:9. After spending nearly one hour with her, I asked her if she would read the scripture to herself and then share with me what she was feeling. She read the verse to herself and looked up and said that she could see that she, as a missionary, should fast and pray often. I told her that was a great observation but that I was asking what she felt. I asked her again to read and share her feelings.

---

13. Boyd K. Packer, "Reverence Invites Revelation," *Ensign*, Nov. 1991.

Again she read and then shared another observation about how to be a better missionary. I agreed that it was a wonderful observation, but I wanted her to share a feeling. Again I asked her to read and then share a feeling. After about the fourth time of her providing observations and me asking her to read again and share a feeling, I could see some frustration on her face. I then said, "You are probably wondering what word or words I want to hear from you. You are thinking that I am trying to pull something from you and you do not know what it is. But I am not. In fact, I do not know what to expect. I only know when it happens, and it has not happened yet. Please be patient with me. Would you mind reading the scripture again to yourself and then sharing what you are feeling?" She said, "I will try one more time."

When she finished, and after some silence, she looked at me and said, "I feel I need to repent." We had arrived.

I asked her, "Why, what is wrong?" She shared with me that she had not been very nice to her companion. I then asked, "So what are you going to do about it?" With tears flowing down her cheeks, she said, almost inaudibly, "I am going to love her." At this point the Spirit filled the room as never before. This sister received revelation. She learned of her actions, and more important, she learned how to correct them.

The experience with this sister was not unique. I have many similar stories. Here is one more:

An elder and I read and studied a scripture together. As with the sister above, after studying the scripture, I asked him to read it silently and then share a feeling. After several attempts, the Spirit filled the room. I knew that he had a personal revelation, but unlike others, he did not share it with me. The two of us sat in complete silence. I perceived it was not that he could not share it but that he did not want to share it. Then it became clear what his thoughts were. The Spirit spoke to me these words: "He doubts that he should be serving a mission." Upon receiving that, I said to him, "You have doubts that you should be here at the MTC." As those words left my mouth, his eyes filled with tears. Overcome with emotion, he was unable to speak, so he gave a simple affirmative nod.

After he gained his composure, I again asked what he was feeling, and he said, "I am at the right place and at the right time."

Please note that in both situations studying and pondering the scriptures was the gate to revelation. It came because they were living the commandments to their best ability and—united with study, prayer, and being still and knowing He is God (D&C 101:16)—they received precious insight and help; they received personal revelation.

Elder Oaks has said, "The word of the Lord in the scriptures is like a lamp to guide our feet (see Psalm 119:105), and revelation is like a mighty force that increases the lamp's illumination manyfold. We encourage everyone to make careful study of the scriptures and of the prophetic teachings concerning them and to prayerfully seek personal revelation to know their meaning for themselves."[14]

Revelation is a gift, and how we treat that gift demonstrates our seriousness and eagerness to receive more. If our personal revelations are of great worth, then we must not set them at naught and trample them under our feet (see 1 Nephi 19:7). As we receive personal revelation, it should be recorded.

Elder David A. Bednar suggested that we "write [our] thoughts and feelings." He then continued:

> Recording what we learn and writing about what we think and feel as we study the scriptures helps us to revisit the same spirit that brought the initial insight or revelation and invites even greater understanding than was originally received. Recording our learnings and writing about our thoughts and feelings is another form of pondering and of always remembering him and is an invitation to the Holy Ghost for continued instruction.
>
> I personally bear testimony of the power of this principle. As we take the time to write what we think and feel in relation to studying the scriptures, an additional and increased outpouring of insight will come.[15]

Receiving revelation and recording it along with insights and feelings is vital to studying the scriptures. The problem with keeping notes is the difficulty of referring to them in the future. The Gospel Library solves that problem. Your notes are attached to content and combined with excellent search capabilities. Finding your notes is no longer a problem.

The Gospel Library is a wonderful blessing.

---

14. Dallin H. Oaks, "Scripture Reading and Revelation," *Ensign*, Jan. 1995.

15. David A. Bednar, "Understanding the Importance of Scripture Study" (Ricks College devotional, Jan. 6, 1998).

7 Minutes a Day—Really

The previous chapter has stressed the importance of studying the scriptures and the resulting personal revelation.

At this point you may question the idea that scripture study, let alone receiving revelation, can occur in seven minutes. I am going to address each of these issues separately.

STUDYING THE SCRIPTURES

Can one effectively study the scriptures in seven minutes? To answer that question, we must first ask another question: if seven minutes is not enough time, then for how long should one study the scriptures?

President Marion G. Romney and President Ezra Taft Benson both suggested that half an hour was a reasonable amount of time to study.[16]

The above quote is the only one that I have found regarding how long we should study the scriptures. On the other hand, I have found an abundance of comments from the brethren regarding how often we should study.

For example, President Benson said in the same talk, "There is a book we need to study daily, both as individuals and as families, namely the Book of Mormon. I love that book."[17]

Recently I conducted a poll among my contacts throughout the country who are members of the Church. I then asked them to forward the poll to their contacts. In the poll, 76 percent of those that did study the scriptures were not happy with the amount of time they spent studying the scriptures. Interestingly, regardless of the amount of time they studied, most reported they felt it wasn't enough time. The biggest challenge all the respondents had was finding time in their busy schedules to study.

Clearly, the frustration or guilt in studying the scriptures is often related to time, so I am going to temporarily remove time from the equation and look at what steps are involved in studying the scriptures.

---

16. Ezra Taft Benson, "A Sacred Responsibility," *Ensign*, May 1986.
17. Benson, "A Sacred Responsibility."

1. Pray for understanding, and ask any specific question you may have.
2. Ask questions as you read.
3. Ponder what you have read.
4. Record your feelings and thoughts.
5. Close with prayer, expressing your gratitude and asking for help as needed, and then listen.

Now let's bring time back in. There are two points in every time line: the start and the end. Of the two, the former is not only the most important but also the only one we should concern ourselves with; when to end will take care of itself.

START WITH SEVEN MINUTES

I suggest that if you are struggling to find the time to study the scriptures, start with seven minutes.

Anyone can find seven minutes within the day. I have found that seven minutes is enough time to have prayer, study, ponder, and write your thoughts. If you run over or under a little bit, that is okay.

In 2000, Malcolm Gladwell's book *The Tipping Point: How Little Things Can Make a Big Difference* was published and became a best seller. Gladwell introduced groundbreaking insight to how trends become popular using the popularity of Hush Puppies, a very popular shoe in the mid-1990s, and the dramatic drop of the crime rate in New York City during the same time period as examples.

He identified three distinguishing characteristics to explain how the trends started. It is the second characteristic that concerns us. He said, "The second distinguishing characteristic of these two examples is that in both cases *little changes had big effects*. All of the possible reasons for why New York's crime rate dropped are changes that happened at the margin; they were *incremental changes*."[18]

Though not a member of the Church, he unwittingly provided modern examples of what Alma told Helaman, that "by small and simple things are great things brought to pass" (Alma 37:6).

President Oaks mentions how "small and simple things" applies to studying the scriptures. Said he, "[There] is the powerful effect over time

---

18. Malcom Gladwell, *The Tipping Point: How Little Things Can Make a Big Difference*, (New York: Little, Brown and Company, 2000) 8; emphasis added.

of the small and simple things we are taught in the scripture and by living prophets. *Consider the scripture study we've been taught to incorporate into our daily lives.* Or consider the personal prayers and the kneeling family prayers that are regular practices for faithful Latter-day Saints. Consider attendance at seminary for youth or institute classes for young adults. Though each of these practices may seem to be small and simple, over time they result in powerful spiritual uplift and growth. This occurs because each of these small and simple things invites the companionship of the Holy Ghost, the Testifier who enlightens us and guides us into truth."[19]

Yes, seven minutes can be effective.

What is important is that you start and do the best you can. As President Nelson reminded us when he spoke at Safeco Field in Seattle, Washington, "The Lord likes effort. . . . He blesses effort."[20]

As you get in the daily habit of studying—not just reading—through your faith and prayers and study of the scriptures, the Holy Ghost will guide you to find the appropriate amount of time you need in your circumstances and provide a way for you to manage your schedule and demands in life more effectively. Daily scripture study will become a meaningful event that will occur without frustration or guilt and change your life.

I am very hesitant to suggest how to use the seven minutes because it should be guided by the Spirit. However, as an example, you could do the following:

- 1 minute of prayer
- 4 minutes of reading / marking text / raising questions
- 2 minutes of prayer, listening, and recording

There may be times that you find yourself doing the following:

- 3 minutes of prayer
- 2 minutes of reading / marking text
- 2 minutes of recording an impression

How the time is used is of little concern as long as you engage in prayer, study, and listening to the Spirit.

Our Heavenly Father understands that you are a work in progress. His main concern is that you are headed in the right direction; even if it's

---

19. Dallin H. Oaks, "Small and Simple Things," *Ensign*, May 2018; emphasis added.
20. Russell M. Nelson, "Lessons Life Has Taught Me," September 2018.

seven minutes at a time. As you act with faith and learn from revelation, you will move forward and, over time, learn what works best for you.

So be good to yourself and just do the best you can.

KEY TO EFFECTIVE STUDY

The key to making scripture study a part of your busy life is your mobile device. Your smartphone is always with you. It provides you with quick access, any time during the day, to the scriptures and a full library of study material that includes videos, manuals, talks, magazines, and more.

In addition, the tools in the Library provide unique ways to drink deeply from the scriptures, organize, and record what you have learned. One of the goals of this book is to help you learn to effectively use these tools.

REVELATION

Revelation cannot be forced; it comes according to the Lord's timetable. It comes from doing what we can to live the commandments and covenants we have made.

Though it comes on the Lord's timetable, it *will* come, and it can come daily. Lorenzo Snow said, "This is the grand privilege of every Latter-day Saint. We know that it is our right to have manifestations of the Spirit every day of our lives."[21]

However, there are times that I feel the heavens are closed. Sometimes at the end of my scripture study revelation does not come, at least not immediately.

President Nelson in the April 2018 general conference counseled us, "To be sure, there may be times when you feel as though the heavens are closed. But I promise that as you continue to be obedient, expressing gratitude for every blessing the Lord gives you, and as you patiently honor the Lord's timetable, you will be given the knowledge and understanding you seek."

While revelation may not come immediately to me, I always feel the Spirit. I feel at peace. I feel what Alma spoke of when he said, "he did speak peace to our souls, and did grant unto us great faith" (Alma 58:11).

---

21. Lorenzo Snow, *Teachings of Presidents of the Church* (2012), 76.

Often we receive revelation, but it comes in small bits, fleeting thoughts that appear insignificant, and so we ignore them. This is why it is important to record your feelings and thoughts as they pass through your mind.

Sensitivity to the Spirit is like a muscle and must be developed over time. President Boyd K. Packer said, "I have learned that strong, impressive spiritual experiences do not come very frequently."[22] Elder Bednar then added, "Most typically we receive a series of seemingly small and incremental spiritual impressions and nudges, which in totality constituencies the desired confirmation about the correctness of the path which we are pursuing."[23]

My point is simple. Do not judge the effectiveness of studying for seven minutes based on if you receive revelation at the end of your studying. Revelation comes on the Lord's timetable, not yours—but it will come, and it often comes in pieces.

That is why it is important to write down whatever you are feeling or thoughts you may have, no matter how insignificant they may appear at the time. Answers will come over the next few hours, days, or weeks. They will come, as Elder Bednar stated, as "a series of seemingly small and incremental spiritual impressions and nudges."[24] So we need to be careful to not dismiss a fleeting thought. We need to record it; it may be the seed of an answer to a prayer or question.

Lastly, we need to give thanks when we receive revelation. Best we remember that "he who receiveth all things with thankfulness shall be made glorious; and the things of the earth shall be added unto him, even an hundred fold" (D&C 78:19).

Certainly, the words of Cicero ring true: "Gratitude is not only the greatest of virtues, but the parent of all others."[25]

---

22. Boyd K. Packer, "The Candle of the Lord," *Ensign*, Jan. 1983.

23. David A. Bednar, "Line upon Line, Precept upon Precept" (Brigham Young University–Idaho devotional, Sept. 2001).

24. Bednar, "Line upon Line."

25. Cicero, 106–43 BCE.

SUMMARY

In summary, seven minutes can be sufficient; it can be a starting point for many wonderful blessings in your life because "by small and simple things are great things brought to pass" (Alma 37:6).

Your mobile device will enable you to make the most of your time studying.

Revelation is real and available to all those who seek it and have patience in receiving it. We have been promised that those who can "wait upon the Lord shall renew their strength . . . [and] shall inherit the earth" (Isaiah 40:31, Psalms 37:9). With patience you will receive "revelations in [your] time" (D&C 59:4).

The Lord Has
Prepared the Way

As previously mentioned, one reason seven minutes can work is that the technology you hold in your hand is always available and provides you with all the materials you need to effectively study the scriptures.

Within your hands are all of the scriptures along with hundreds of other written sources, such as manuals and handbooks, several hundred videos, all the conference talks since January 1971, and all of the *Ensign*, *New Era*, *Friend*, and *Liahona* articles since January 1971.

Yes, we live in a marvelous age. Isaiah said, "[The Lord] will proceed to do a marvelous work . . . even a marvelous work and a wonder" (Isaiah 29:14).

President Joseph Fielding Smith makes it clear that what Isaiah saw was the work in these latter-days. He said, "This marvelous work is the restoration of the Church and the Gospel with all the power and authority, keys and blessings which pertain to this great work for the salvation of the children of men."[26]

We are blessed to be living during these last days, to see the words of Isaiah fulfilled and continue to come to life as the work goes forth until "the earth shall be full of the knowledge of the Lord, as the waters cover the sea" (Isaiah 11:9).

Technological advancements are making it possible for the words of Isaiah to be fulfilled.

Elder David A. Bednar said, "The Lord is hastening His work, and it is no coincidence that these powerful communication innovations and the inventions are occurring in the dispensation of the fulness of times."[27]

Latter-day prophets have long recognized the value of science in hastening the work of the Lord. President Brigham Young stated, "Every discovery in science and art that is really true and useful to mankind has been given by direct revelation from God, though but few acknowledge it. It has been given with a view to prepare the way for the ultimate

---

26. Joseph Fielding Smith, *Church History and Modern Revelation* 1:35.
27. David A. Bednar, "To Sweep the Earth as with a Flood," BYU Campus Education Week, Aug. 19, 2014.

triumph of truth, and the redemption of the earth from the power of sin and Satan."[28]

Evidence of Young's statement was seen in advancements in transportation and communications. As the gospel spreads throughout the world, the Lord has provided other means for His anointed to traverse the earth and to speak to the world as a whole. Today we can hear the voice of His servants using a smartphone; this is not the result of happenstance.

Joseph Fielding Smith stated, "I maintain that had there been no restoration of the gospel, and no organization of The Church of Jesus Christ of Latter-day Saints, there would have been no radio . . . and the many other things wherein the world has been benefited by such discoveries. Under such conditions these blessing would have been withheld, for they belong to the Dispensation of the Fulness of Times for which the restoration of the gospel and the organization of the Church constitute the central point, from which radiates the Spirit of the Lord through the world. The inspiration of the Lord has gone out and takes hold of the minds of men, though they know it not, and they are directed by the Lord. In this manner he brings them into his service that his purposes and his righteousness, in due time, may be supreme on the earth. Now let me say briefly that I do not believe for one moment that these discoveries have come by chance, or they have come because of superior intelligence possessed by men today over those who lived in ages that are past. They have come and are coming because the time is ripe, because the Lord has willed it, and because he has poured out his Spirit on all flesh."[29]

In April 1974, President Spencer W. Kimball addressed regional representatives. In his talk "When the World Will Be Converted" he stated, "I believe that the Lord is anxious to put into our hands inventions of which we laymen have hardly had a glimpse."

During that same year, personal computers were introduced. Among the entries were the IBM 5100 and the TRS-80 Commodore PET. A year later, two visionaries, Bill Gates and Paul Allen, formed a company called Microsoft, and in 1976 Steve Jobs, Paul Wozniak, and Ronald Wayne introduced the Apple I.

Just five years later, the term "personal computer" came into being with IBM's introduction of the IBM 5150. It weighed in at over fifty

---

28. Brigham Young, *Journal of Discourses*, 9:369, Aug. 31, 1862.
29. Joseph Fielding Smith, in Conference Report, Oct. 1926, 117.

pounds, had two floppy drives and 40K of read-only memory with 16K of user memory, and sold for $1,565; in today's dollars, that would be over $4,200. Today we carry in our pockets computer power far beyond the IBM 5150 at a fraction of the cost.

President Gordon B. Hinckley expressed, "We are confident that as the work of the Lord expands, he will inspire men to develop the means whereby the membership of the Church . . . can be counseled in an intimate and personal way by his chosen prophet."[30] Two years later, the makings of the internet began, and in 1996 two Stanford University students, Sergey Brin and Larry Page, developed the Google search engine, opening to the world access to information overload.

The ubiquitous presence of mobile devices has changed how the world searches for knowledge. In May of 2015, Google reported there are more searches now on mobile devices than on desktop computers.[31]

The use of mobile devices has greatly increased. In 1985 the number of cellphone subscribers was a little over 340 thousand,[32] less than 1 percent of the United States population. In 2000 the number of subscribers increased to over 109 million (ibid.), about 39 percent of the population.

According to the Pew Research Center, as of January 2018, 95 percent of American adults own a cell phone, and 77 percent of those have a smartphone. Tablet ownership also continues to increase. Currently over 50 percent of American adults own a tablet,[33] and these numbers will continue to increase as technology advances and makes them easier to use.

Clearly the Lord is providing a way for us to be "abounding in good works" (Mosiah 5:15) and "feasting upon the word of Christ" (2 Nephi 31:20) that we may "give attendance to reading, to exhortation, to doctrine" (1 Timothy 4:13) and that "the earth shall be full of the knowledge of the Lord, as the waters cover the sea" (Isaiah 11:9). It is to that end that we have been blessed not only with technology but also the means to use

---

30. Gordon B. Hinckley, "Faith: The Essence of True Religion," *Ensign*, Nov. 1981.

31. Greg Sterling, *It's Official: Google Says More Searches Now on Mobile than on Desktop*, SearchEngineLand, 2015, http://searchengineland.com/its-official-google-says-more-searches-now-on-mobile-than-on-desktop-220369.

32. *Cell Phone Subscribers in the U.S., 1985–2010, Infoplease* http://www.infoplease.com/ipa/A0933563.htm.

33. Pew Research Center, *Mobile Fact Sheet*, Feb. 5, 2018, http://www.pewinternet.org/fact-sheets/mobile-technology-fact-sheet.

that technology to enrich our study of the gospel, enhance our teaching, and more effectively engage in missionary work.

He has provided us with a wonderful tool, the Gospel Library. I again repeat what Elder Golden said about the Gospel Library: "The Church has dedicated significant effort to improve this app in order to support Church members as they seek to increase their gospel learning and inspiration using mobile devices. **We encourage members to use it to enhance their study and draw near to the Lord and His holy prophets.**"[34]

---

34. Christoffel Golden Jr., "Major Upgrade for Gospel Library App for iOS Devices Announced," *Church News*, June 25, 2013; emphasis added.

SECTION TWO

Introduction to the Tools

One of the problems of recording personal revelation is retrieving it in the future; personal revelation recorded and forgotten or lost is of little use. We need to build upon what has been revealed previously, and the Gospel Library provides that means. In addition, the Gospel Library provides us the tools to connect in meaningful ways to the scriptures that were never thought possible.

Take the time to learn how to use the Gospel Library. If you prayerfully use it daily with a desire to learn how to use it effectively and to hasten His work, in a very short time, you will realize great blessings, your understanding of the gospel will deepen, and your effectiveness as a teacher and missionary will increase as you are directed by the Spirit.

Several years ago, I was involved in a discussion about the Gospel Library with a member of the Church. He responded that he had tried several times to use his iPad in studying the scriptures but always returned to his old tried-and-true printed copy.

I gave him my iPad and invited him to take some time to see how I use the Gospel Library in my scripture study. Later we met, and he said, "I have had one of the most spiritual experiences in my life." I was taken aback by the comment and was curious and excited to hear what happened. He then said, "The first thing I did when I opened the Gospel Library in your iPad was turn to the fifth chapter of Jacob, and I was amazed what you did. I now see the value of using the Gospel Library; I am converted."

More recently someone shared with me how much more they enjoyed studying the scriptures now that they have learned to use the Gospel Library.

As stated previously, Elder Christoffel Golden Jr. said, "The Church has dedicated significant effort to improve [the Gospel Library] in order to support Church members as they seek to increase their gospel learning and inspiration using mobile devices. **We encourage members to use it to enhance their study and draw near to the Lord and His holy prophets.**"[35] Let's look at how the Gospel Library is organized.

The Gospel Library is a compilation of content to aid in studying and teaching the gospel. It provides a set of tools to help use the content. The tools are divided into four categories.

SETTINGS

- **Syncing**—Protect your marked content, notes, tags, links, and notebooks.
- **Customization**—Personalize various aspect of the Gospel Library.

STUDYING

- **Search**—Locate material throughout the Gospel Library and notes. This will aid your studies and help you move about the scriptures quickly.
- **Mark and Style**—Highlight and underline text in various colors.
- **Tag**—Organize the Gospel Library into personal topics or index so that you can quickly retrieve information by topic— similar to hashtags (#) in social media.
- **Note**—Link notes to marked content for them to become part of the related content. The notes are your personal record of revelations, personal insights, or comments by others related to the marked content.
- **Links**—Link related pieces of content across sources.
- **Related Content**—Add to your footnotes. You'll have the footnotes found in the 1985 LDS Edition of the scriptures in Gospel Library, but you can add your own links and notes as well.
- **Define**—Look up definitions with the dictionary built into the app.
- **Maps**—Increase understanding of historical events with additional geographical information.

---

35. "Major Upgrade for Gospel Library App for iOS Devices Announced," *Church News*, June 25, 2013; emphasis added.

ORGANIZATION

- **Bookmarks**—Resume where you left off.
- **Collections**—Locate content easily with the categories listed on the main screen.
- **Multi-screens**—Use multi-screens to help you move quickly from screen to screen, similar to tabs in a browser.
- **Notebook**—Organize ideas, impressions, talks, or lessons. The notebook has notes, which are the equivalent of pages and are not to be confused with notes in the study section.
- **History**—Move back or forth within the content that has been previously viewed.

EDITING

- **Edit**—Make changes in content you have created.
- **Duplicate**—Copy content to a notebook of your choice.
- **Copy**—Move annotated content outside the Gospel Library and paste elsewhere.
- **Delete**—Remove notes, tags, and links you have created, but NOT the marked text.
- **Remove**—Remove marked text AND any attached links, notes, and tags.

Customizing the
Gospel Library

Before getting started, let's make sure that your work is syncing and you have customized your settings.

SYNCING

Sync all your notes, notebooks, tags, links, and marked content online so that everything you create in the Gospel Library is saved. This protects you against losing work if your device crashes, and it allows you to work across multiple devices—for example, between your smartphone and tablet. The Gospel Library uses the term *syncing*, but you can also look at this as providing you with a backup. Technically there are differences, but for this book "syncing" and "backing up" are synonymous.

NOVICE

You must have an LDS Account. If you do not have one, do the following:

- In your browser, go to lds.org.
- Click on "My Account and Ward."
- Click on "Sign In."
- Click on "Register for an LDS Account."
- Click on "Register as a Member" (if you are a member of The Church of Jesus Christ of Latter-day Saints) OR click on "Register as a Friend."
- Complete the requested information to complete registration.

To make sure you are syncing, go to the Gospel Library app:

iOS
- Tap on the settings icon.
- Under LDS Account should be your username. If not, log in.

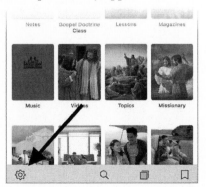

Android

- Tap on the option menu icon.
- Tap on Settings.
- Under LDS Account should be your username. If not, log in.

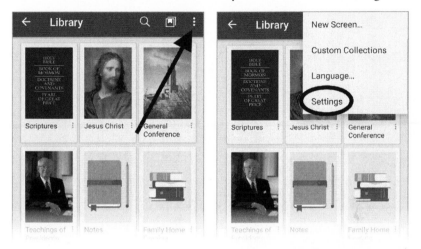

If you see you user name, you are signed in. You will also see under your user name "Last Sync:" (time last synced).

If you do not see your username:

- Tap on Sign in.
- Enter your LDS Account username.
- Enter your LDS Account password.

PHONES

To sync your device, you must have access to the Church servers. It can either be through Wi-Fi or using cellular data.

If it is through Wi-Fi, then your phone will only sync when you have access to Wi-Fi. If you use your cellular connection, then the Gospel Library will sync each time you create content.

If you have an unlimited data plan with your carrier, it is best to allow the Gospel Library to use cellular data so that the Gospel Library is always up to date and syncing. Contact your carrier for information about your plan and consequences of allowing the Gospel Library to use cellular data.

The Gospel Library requires you to give permission to use cellular data. To give permission you need to leave the Gospel Library and go to your phone settings:

iOS

* Settings / Library / Cellular Data / On

Android

- Settings / Apps / Gospel Library / Mobile data / Allow app while Data saver on / On

If that did not work, then try:

- Settings / General / Apps / Gospel Library / App Info / Data / Background Data / On

Note: Keep in mind that with Android there are different phone models and software versions. Above I have shown the procedure for a Galaxy

S9 and an LG respectively. If you have a problem finding the settings, search Google or contact your carrier.

Note: The syncing process involves all devices regardless of the type, make, and model of your device. For example, if you have an iPhone and an Android tablet, the Gospel Library will sync between the two devices.

TABLETS

Most people do not have a cellular plan for their tablets. If you do have cellular access, then your content will be continually synced if you have given permission. If you do not have a cellular plan, then your tablet will be synced when you have access to Wi-Fi.

If your tablet does not have a cellular plan, then there is a problem that can occur if you use the Gospel Library on two different devices (for example, your phone and a tablet).

This most often happens when you use your tablet and mark content without having Wi-Fi access available at the time you are using the Gospel Library.

Later you use your smartphone and study the same material and see that the content is not marked (because the tablet has not been able to sync), so you mark the same content again. Once the tablet does sync, that content will have been marked twice; once with the tablet and once with the phone.

This is not the end of the world and is easily corrected. More about this will be discussed in the chapter on marking scriptures.

WARNING WARNING

Yes, this deserves two warnings.

Regardless of what or how many devices you have, check every week or so to make sure they are syncing. If your device crashes and your Gospel Library has not been syncing, you will lose all your work from the time of the last sync up to the crash.

INTERMEDIATE

Make sure your device is syncing, and if it is not, sign in. If your tablet does not have cellular data, then it will sync the next time you are in an area where you have Wi-Fi access.

Unless you are on a limited data plan, I suggest you give Gospel Library permission to use cellular data. See the steps above on how to do that.

Check a few times each month to make sure you are syncing.

ADVANCED

Make sure you allow the Gospel Library to have access to your cellular data if you have an unlimited data plan. Check a few times a month to make sure you are syncing.

• •

PERSONALIZATION

In the app's settings, you can personalize a few things, such as the font size and color scheme.

NOVICE

There is not much to do here except open your settings and follow along with the explanations below. This chapter is divided into two sections, one for iOS and one for Android.

iOS

LDS ACCOUNT

- *Sign in*—Do this as mentioned in the previous section so that all your devices are synced on the Church servers.

FEEDBACK

- *Send Feedback*—Communicate easily with the developers of the Gospel Library. It is vital that they hear from you. You can share with them possible bugs, ideas, or comments. When you tap on Send Feedback, the feedback screen opens.
  - » Type in your name. I know it is optional, but let's be friendly. Your first name will suffice. You only need to do this once.
  - » Type in your email address. You only need to do this once.

> » Tap on Category, and then tap on the category that best fits your situation.
>
> » Provide a description about the bug, your ideas, or your comments. You can use up to one thousand characters, so make sure your description is clear. Explain the steps you took and what kinds of problems you noticed.
>
> » In the lower left-hand corner is a paperclip icon. Tap on that if you have a screenshot. Screenshots are very helpful. If you have a problem, such as a frozen screen or some other odd behavior, take a screenshot and send it with your comments.
>
> » Tap on the paperclip icon, and choose the picture(s) you want to send. You can send more than one.
>
> » Tap on "Submit" when you're ready to send your feedback.

Once you send the email, you will receive an auto acknowledgment almost immediately. The email goes to service missionaries who read the email and answer questions if possible. If it is a bug you are reporting, then it is sent on to the developers.

Unless your email is asking for help, you will only receive the auto acknowledgment. If you are looking for some help, then you should receive a response within a day or two.

CONTENT

- *Language*—Pick a language of your choice. Not all languages have all the standard works in the Library or all the Church materials translated, but they all have the Book of Mormon.
- *Downloaded Media*—Find videos you have downloaded here.

DISPLAY

- *Text Size*—Adjust the text size to what is comfortable for you. As you move the slide to the right, the text gets larger. Below the slide is an example of how the text will look.
- *Theme*—Choose the color you prefer to work with. There are currently five choices. As you pick the color, the menu bar will change to the color you picked.
- *List Mode*—Decide if you want the Library collections shown as icons or as a list.

- *Hide Footnotes*—Turn off footnotes if seeing the references in the text bothers you. This does not impact related content or the footnotes found in the related content. Normally you would see the following in a scripture:

having dwelt at ᶜJerusalem

The text in the Gospel Library is colored to show it is a hyperlink to a footnote. If you hide the footnotes, this is what you will see:

having dwelt at Jerusalem

This setting is useful if you are going to use the copy function because the superscript is lost in the copying process. Using the above example, if you copied and pasted the text above into another document without turning on Hide Footnotes, it would look like this:

having dwelt at cJerusalem

Note: Whenever you switch the Hide Footnotes option on or off, you need to close the Gospel Library and then open it again for the switch to take effect.

- *Allow Fullscreen*—Hide the menu bar so that there are no distractions when you are reading. For the menu bar to reappear, tap anywhere on the screen.

ADDITIONAL SETTINGS

- *Featured Apps*—Look at a list of other apps by the Church. They are all excellent apps.
- *Advanced*
  - » *Allow In-App Notifications*—Allow a notification to appear when you open the Gospel Library (for example, an announcement that a new video is available). Obviously, this is not a daily occurrence.
  - » *Show Obsolete Content*—View annual items, like old outlines for sharing times, old curriculum, old manuals, and seasonal items.
  - » *Use Cellular data for Content Updates*—Receive automatic updates of the Gospel Library catalog and books when this

function is enabled. This will usually take place when you open the app.

- *About*—Access all the legal information that no one reads: Rights and Use Information and the Privacy Policy. However, if you tap on Acknowledgments, the first paragraph mentions the 1Password extension.

1Password is an excellent password protection app. I highly recommend it. I use it myself. If you are relying on sticky notes, a small spiral notebook, or your memory to store all your passwords, you need to change your ways.

If you do not need an app to help with your passwords because your password is short and easy to remember—maybe the name of your dog, cat, or a grandchild?—then you need 1Password.

1Password will create excellent passwords for you, remember them, and automatically paste them in your app or website. If you use 1Password with the Gospel Library, 1Password will enter your username and password for you after you have identified yourself using your thumbprint or face identification or a master password.

There are other password apps out there, such as Dashlane or LastPass.

ANDROID

LDS ACCOUNT

- *Sign in*—Do this as mentioned in the previous section so all your devices are synced on the Church servers.

CONTENT

- *Downloaded Media*—Find videos you have downloaded here.
- *Limit Mobile Network Use*—Turn this on if you would like to limit your phone's ability to download content when using Wi-Fi.

DISPLAY

- *Theme*—Choose the color you prefer to work with. There are currently five choices. As you pick the color, the menu bar will change to the color you picked.
- *Text Size*—Adjust the text size to what is comfortable for you. As you move the slide to the right, the text gets larger. Below the slide is an example of how the text will look.
- *List Mode*—Decide if you want the Library collections shown as icons or as a list.
- *Hide Footnotes*—Turn off footnotes if seeing the references in the text bothers you. This does not impact related content. Normally you would see the following in a scripture:

> having dwelt at ᵃJerusalem

If you hide the footnotes, this is what you will see:

> having dwelt at Jerusalem

This setting is useful if you are going to use the copy function because the superscript is lost in the copying process. Using the above example, if you copied and pasted the text above into another document without turning on Hide Footnotes, it would look like this:

> having dwelt at cJerusalem

- *Show Screens as Separate Windows*—Run multiple windows in a split screen (depending on the version of Android you are running).
- *Show Obsolete Content*—View annual items, like old outlines for sharing times, old curriculum, old manuals, and seasonal items.
- *Allow In-App Notifications*—Allow a notification to appear when you open the Gospel Library (for example, an announcement that a new video is available). Obviously, this is not a daily occurrence.

ADDITIONAL SETTINGS

- *Featured Apps*—Look at a list of other apps by the Church. They are all excellent apps.

- *Send Feedback*—Communicate easily with the developers of the Gospel Library. It is vital that they hear from you. You can share with them possible bugs, ideas, or comments. When you tap on Send Feedback, the feedback screen opens.

  » Type in your name. I know it is optional, but let's be friendly. Your first name will suffice. You only need to do this once.

  » Type in your email address. You only need to do this once.

  » Tap on Category, and then tap on the category that best fits your situation.

  » Provide a description about the bug, your ideas, or your comments. You can use up to one thousand characters, so make sure your description is clear. Explain the steps you took and what kinds of problems you noticed.

  » In the lower left-hand corner is a paperclip icon. Tap on that if you have a screenshot. Screenshots are very helpful. If you have a problem, such as a frozen screen or some other odd behavior, take a screenshot and send it with your comments.

  » Tap on the paperclip icon, and choose the picture(s) you want to send. You can send more than one.

  » Tap on "Submit" when you're ready to send your feedback.

  Once you send the email, you will receive an auto acknowledgment almost immediately. The email goes to service missionaries who read the email and answer questions if possible. If it is a bug you are reporting, then it is sent on to the developers.

  Unless your email is asking for help, you will only receive the auto acknowledgment. If you are looking for some help, then you should receive a response within a day or two.

- *About*—Access all the legal information that no one reads: Rights and Use Information, Privacy Policy, and Acknowledgments. This section also shows what version of the app you have.

Engaging in Meaningful Study & Research

The next set of tools is to help you make the most of your reading, studying, and research.

Each chapter introduces a new tool and starts with a Novice section, which can be completed in seven minutes or less. Make sure you understand how to use the tool before moving on. Some chapters have a Going Deeper section. Proceed to that section when you feel you are ready. Then, as your confidence increases, read the intermediate and advanced sections.

For intermediate and advanced, go to the end of the chapter for a section geared toward your skill level. However, it would not hurt for you to also quickly skim through the Novice section before reading your section.

Day 1: Searching for Scriptures

Quickly locate a scripture

(**7 MINUTES**)

NOVICE

Study—remember to start and end with prayer.

- Tap on the search icon (which is available from any screen).

iOS

Android

- Make sure the search field is empty. If it is not empty, tap on the cancel icon.

You are going to search for Matthew 5:48. You type only the first letter of the book (m), followed by the chapter number (5), followed by the verse (48). You do not need any spaces.

- Type "m548" (without the quotes) in the search field.
- **Do not** tap on the search key on the keyboard. That key is for finding words or phrases
- Scroll down the list of scriptures until you see Matthew 5:48.

- Tap on Matthew 5:48.

You are now at Matthew 5:48. Read and ponder the verse.

- Tap on the search icon.
- Make sure the search field is empty.
- If it is not empty, tap on the cancel icon.
- Type "n1248" for Nephi (n) chapter 12, verse 48.
- Scroll down the list below until you see "3 Nephi 12:48."
- Tap on "3 Nephi 12:48."

You are now at 3 Nephi 12:48. Read and ponder the verse. What was different between the two verses? Not sure?

Here is how to switch back and forth between the two verses.

iOS

- Tap on the bookmark icon.
- Tap on History at the top of the list.
- Tap on Matthew 5.

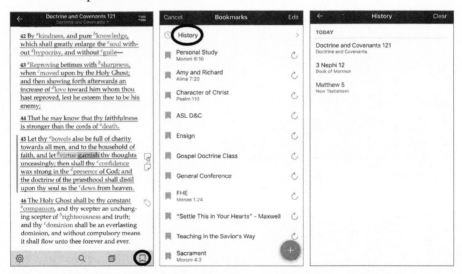

You are now back to Matthew 5:48.

- Tap on the bookmark icon.
- Tap on History.
- Tap on 3 Nephi 12.

You are now back to 3 Nephi 12:48.

Repeat the above process to move back and forth between the two scriptures. In Chapter 13, I will cover other methods to move back and forth among content.

Android
- Tap on the bookmark icon.
- Tap on History.
- Tap on Matthew 5.

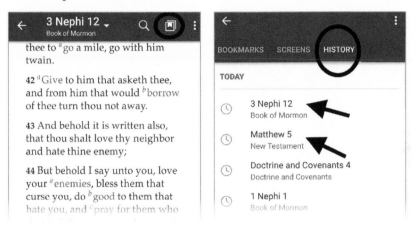

You are now back to Matthew 5:48.

- Tap on the bookmark icon.
- Tap on History.
- Tap on 3 Nephi 12.

You are now back to 3 Nephi 12:48.

THINGS TO REMEMBER

- No spaces are needed.
- Make sure the search field is empty.
- Type the first letter of the book.
- Type the chapter number.
- Type the verse (optional).

For the Doctrine and Covenants, just type a "d" followed by the section number and verse.

REMEMBER

When searching for a scripture, **do not** tap on the search key on the keyboard. That key is for finding words or phrases.

INTERMEDIATE

- Tap on the search icon.
- Make sure the search field is empty. If it is not empty, tap on the cancel icon.
- Type "m528."
- Scroll down the list until you see Matthew 5:48.
- Tap on Matthew 5:48.

You do not need to enter a verse if you want to start at the beginning of a chapter. For Matthew chapter 5, type "m5." For the Doctrine and Covenants, just type a "d" followed by the section number.

ADVANCED

Searching for a scripture is easy. To find Matthew 5:38, type without spaces "m528." To search just for the chapter, type "m5." Type "d43" for Doctrine and Covenants 4:3 or Doctrine and Covenants 43.

Day 2: Searching for a Word or Phrase

Quickly find a word or phrase
throughout the Gospel Library

7 MINUTES

NOVICE

SEARCH FOR A WORD

Study—remember to start and end with prayer.

- Tap on the search icon.
- Make sure the search field is empty. If it is not empty, then tap the cancel icon.
- Type "baptize."
- Tap on the search key on the keyboard.
- Tap on Scriptures.
- Tap on New Testament.
- Tap on Matthew 3.

At the bottom of the screen, it shows "1 of 7 matches."

- Tap on the down arrow several times and observe that the word "baptize" and "baptized" are both selected.

iOS   *Android*

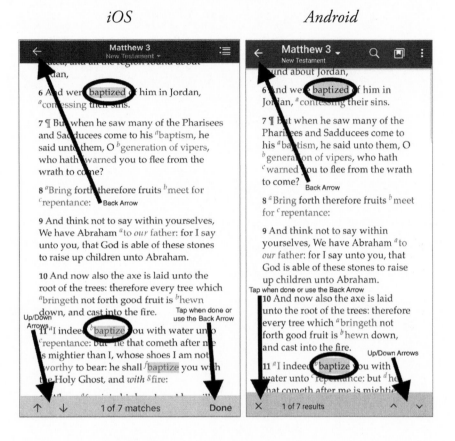

- Use the up and down arrows to find verse 11. Read and ponder the verse.

iOS

- Tap on Done.
- Tap on the search icon.
- Tap on the next scripture—Matthew 20.
- Read and ponder the verses that contain "baptize."

Android

- Tap on the cancel icon.
- Tap on the back icon.
- Tap on the next scripture—Matthew 20.
- Read and ponder the verses that contain "baptize."

SEARCH FOR A PHRASE

- Tap on the search icon.
- Make sure the search field is empty.
- If it is not empty, tap the cancel icon.
- Type "gift of the holy ghost" (without the quotes).
- Tap on the search key on the keyboard.
- Tap on Scriptures.

Note: At the time of this printing, Android has added subtopics across the top. Swipe left to see all of them, and tap on "Scriptures" in the subtopics.

- Tap on New Testament.

Notice "Exact Phrase" at the top of the list, and then further down is "Keywords." (You will have to scroll down a little to see it.)

- Tap on the scripture in the list, which is Acts 2.
- Tap on the down arrow to see verse 38.
- Read and ponder the scripture.

Continue checking other scriptures as time permits.

Notice as you and go back and forth from the search function and checking on the references found in the result field, the references you have previously read become grayed out. That is to help you remember what you have already read.

CAPITALIZATION DOES NOT AFFECT THE SEARCH

One thing that the Gospel Library has in common with Google is capitalization is not considered during a search.

INTERMEDIATE

- Tap on the search icon.
- Type the word or phrase you are searching.
- Tap on the search key on the keyboard.

SEARCHING FOR A WORD ON A PAGE.

- Go to Matthew 5.
- Tap on the search icon.
- Type "blessed."

Below the word "blessed," you can see the search icon and the words "Find 'Blessed' on page." Tap on that.

You can also search the Gospel Library for a word or phrase that is already on the screen. Select the word or phrase and tap on the search icon in popup menu.

Every occurrence of the phrase in the Gospel Library will be found. This is a quicker and error-free way of searching for a phrase. The same would work for a word search.

MAKE SURE YOUR SPELLING IS CORRECT

This is not like Google search, where you can type a phrase or word and, even if a misspelling occurs, Google makes suggestions. The Gospel Library is not so forgiving. In fact, it is not forgiving at all, so make sure your spelling is correct.

TO LEAVE THE SEARCH FUNCTION AND RETURN TO WHERE YOU STARTED

iOS

While in content
- Tap on the back arrow.

Android

While in content
- Tap on the bookmark icon.
- Tap on History.
- Tap on the name of the content where you started.

NOT CASE SENSITIVE

Searching for Joseph Smith, joseph smith, or JOSEPH SMITH will bring the same results.

IF YOUR SEARCH SHOWS UP EMPTY

1. What is being searched does not exist.
2. There was a misspelling.
3. You did not clear the search field.

ADVANCED

You can search for a word or phrase using the general search function. There is also another search function found in the popup menu after you select some content. First select a word or phrase in the content, and then tap on Search in the popup menu.

> Note: As of the time of this writing, there is a bug in the search function for both iOS and Android. Sometimes when you type a phrase, the search will not find an exact phrase. If you search for a phrase and an exact search is not found, try enclosing the phrase in quotation marks.

> Note: You can also search for a hymn. There are two ways. You can search by hymn number, or you can type in the first few words of the title of the hymn. Then scroll down the list of suggestions to find the hymn. Either method will take you to the Hymns in the Gospel Library, which contain text only. If you also want the music, tap on Open in LDS Music at the top of the lyrics. Make sure that you have downloaded the app "LDS Music" first.

iOS

- For single digits, type the first word of the title (sometimes the second word will be needed).

Day 3: Marking Scriptures

Mark text for emphasis or clarification

(*7 MINUTES*)

NOVICE

Study—remember to start and end with prayer.

- Go to Doctrine and Covenants 4.
- Read the entire section.
- Place your finger on the word "Therefore" in verse 2, and wait for the popup menu to appear.
- Remove your finger.
- Place your finger on the end control point to select more content.
- Drag your finger down to select the entire verse.

iOS   Android

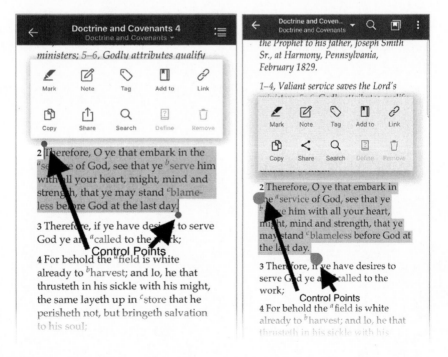

You have just selected some content.

- Tap on Mark.
- Tap on Style.
- Tap on the red icon.
- Tap on the underline icon.

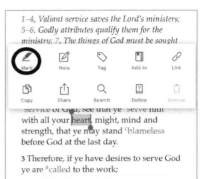

You have now underlined the selected text in red.

Note: Moving the control points does take some steadiness, especially for those with larger fingers, so be patient with yourself.

- Place your finger on the word "heart" in verse 2.
- Tap on Mark then tap on Style.
- Tap on the yellow icon.
- Tap on the highlight icon.
- Tap anywhere on the screen outside of the menu to remove the menu.

You have now highlighted a word in yellow. Now do the above steps for the words "might," "mind," and "strength" in verse 2, choosing a different color for each word.

iOS	*Android*
- Tap anywhere on the screen outside of the menu to remove the menu.	- Tap the check mark.

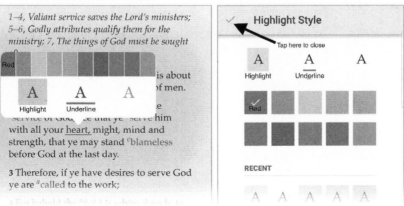

At this point you have learned how to mark content and that you can combine underlining and highlighting. This is not only for marking of scriptures but any text in the Gospel Library (for example, conference talks, manuals, or music).

MAKING CHANGES

Unlike marking in a hard copy of the scriptures, you can change or remove your markings in the Gospel Library.

To make a change in style or color, tap on what you want to change then tap on Style.

- Tap on the word "heart."

A selection menu may appear, asking if you want to work on a highlight or footnote. Tap on Highlight. Now another selection menu appears titled Choose Highlight. Because the highlighted word "heart" and the underlined verse 2 are in close proximity, the app is asking which of the two you want.

iOS *Android*

- Tap on the highlighted word "heart."
- Tap on Style.
- Pick a new color.

Now lets remove the marking.

- Tap on the highlighted word "heart."
- Tap on the word "heart" in the selection menu.
- Tap on Remove.

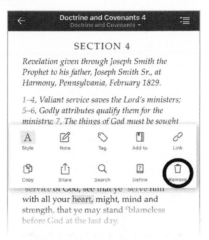

You have now removed the marking for the word "heart." If you had something attached to the marking, for example a note, you would have received a warning that the note will also be removed. Now select the word again and highlight it in a color of your choice.

GOING DEEPER

UH, OH

Sometimes you might mark, in error, the same content more than once with the same color or style; for example, underlining in red the same verse three times. How can that happen?

One way is to mark the same content on more than one device before the devices have had the opportunity to sync. Then, when they sync, the marking has doubled, tripled, etc.

You will know that this has occurred when you try to delete a marking and after tapping on Remove the marking is still there.

iOS

Here is how to solve the problem. Tap on the marked text, and a screen will appear with a list of all the markings and notes that have been made to that selection (see screenshot). Select the first one and remove it, as explained above. Then repeat the process, choosing the next on the list, until all highlights and styles have been deleted.

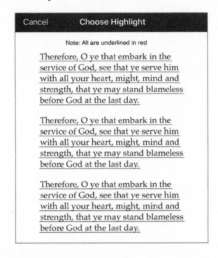

Be careful! Make sure in the process of removing you do not delete any notes, tags, or links you want to keep.

If you see note, tag, or link icons to the right of the marked content, here are the steps you need to follow to avoid deleting the note, tag or link. These steps are only for iOS.

Assume you have a verse underlined in red three times.

- Tap on the verse.
- If asked to select the highlight or footnote, tap Highlight.
- Tap on the first occurrence of red underlining.
- Tap on Style.
- Tap on the yellow icon.
- Tap on the highlight style (the first *A*).
- Tap anywhere on the screen to close.

Now you are going to repeat the above process and pick a different color each time.

After assigning a different color to each occurrence:

- Tap on the verse.
- If asked to select the highlight or footnote, tap Highlight.

You now see that same verse has been highlighted in three different colors.

- Tap on Cancel.
- Tap on the related content icon.

Notice which color has the note, then:

- Tap on the verse.
- If asked to select the highlight or footnote, tap Highlight.
- Tap on one of the other colors that is not attached to the note, and then tap Remove.
- Repeat the process again.

You now have successfully deleted the duplicates without deleting the note.

Android

Android has made it much easier. When you tap on some marked content that you have marked more than once, you will see icons to the left of the text, showing if there is a note or link attached.

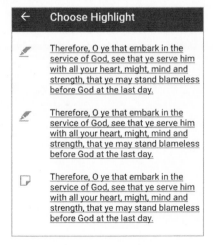

Tap on the content that does not have an attachment, and you're good to go.

INTERMEDIATE

If the content you marked also includes a footnote and later you tap on the marking, you will be asked to indicate which you want.

COMBINING MARKING STYLES

It is possible to combine styles for the same word or phrase. For example, you can underline content and then highlight some of the text in that content as shown below.

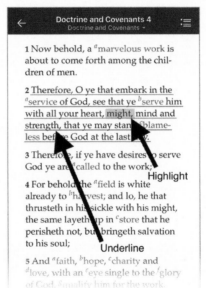

When you combine styles and tap on some marked text, the Gospel Library will usually have trouble knowing which of the marked texts you are referring to. When that happens, you will be asked to indicate which you want to work with. Tap on the one you want, and the popup menu will appear.

ADVANCED

If you remove some highlighting but it is still there, it means that you highlighted the same content in the same color at a different time. One way this happens is when you mark the same content with the same color on more than one device before they have had the chance to sync. Correcting this in iOS requires several steps. To correct this issue in iOS, do the following:

iOS

Tap on the highlighted content, and then tap on Remove. Repeat until they are all removed, but be careful that there isn't something attached to one of them—e.g., a note or tag—that you want to keep. If there is an attachment, tap on the highlighted content and change the color or style. Do this for each instance. Now that you have different colors, you can look in the related content and identify which color has the attachment. Now delete the other highlighting that does not have an attachment.

Android

Correcting the problem is easy because each highlighted content has an icon to the left indicating if a note or link is attached.

You have a choice of ten colors, but the colors can be combined for even more variety. Highlight the content once in one color and then highlight it again in a different color.

Day 4: Notes

Record impressions, revelations, insights, and
comments related to select content

The use of notes while reading is not new. Writing insights and comments on a notepad while reading is an effective way to help digest and remember what you are reading. The problem is retrieving the information at a later date.

Before the digital age, if the note was short, you could write it in the margins. However, in the Gospel Library you have plenty of room to write a note and use the search option to retrieve the note.

7 MINUTES

NOVICE

Study—remember to start and end with prayer.

- Go to 1 Nephi 1:1 and select the word "afflictions."
- Tap on Note.
- In the title, type "Afflictions" (however, this is optional).
- Tap in the body of the note.

iOS   *Android*

- Type in the body the following: "The word comes from the Latin *affligere*, meaning 'infliction of pain or humiliation.'" (This came from a dictionary definition.)
- Tap the return key on the keyboard twice to enter two spaces.
- Now type your thoughts about the word "afflictions." Possibly share some personal experiences.
- Select the word *affigere*.

At the bottom of the note, you have four options that can make your note easier to read: bold, italics, bulleted list, or numbered list.

- Tap on the italics icon.
- Tap on Save (for iOS) or the check mark (for Android).

Note: Did you notice that when you select content and create a note that the selected content is automatically marked in the style you last used to mark text?

- -

GOING DEEPER

HOW TO VIEW THE NOTE

To see the note in the related content:

iOS

- Tap on the related content icon in the upper right-hand corner.

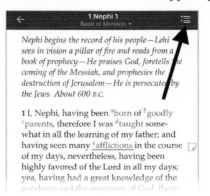

Android

- Tap on the option menu icon.
- Tap on Related Content.

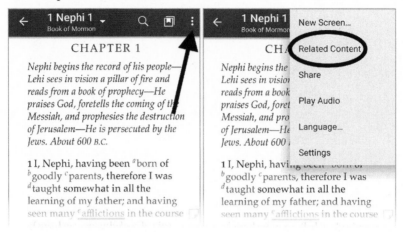

Another option to see the note is by tapping on the note icon in the right-hand margin. This shows only the note without the other items in the related content.

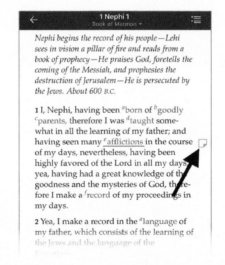

EDITING OR ADDING TO A NOTE

As you read your scriptures, or any other content, there will be times you want to add to a note that you have already created. To demonstrate, you are going to add to the note you created above.

iOS
- Tap on the note icon in the right-hand margin.
- Tap on the option menu icon in the upper right-hand corner.
- Tap Edit Note.
- Add additional text.
- Tap on Save when done.

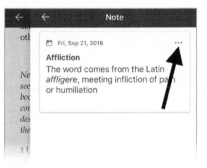

Android
- Tap on the note icon in the right-hand margin.
- Tap on the note.
- Add additional text.
- Tap on the check mark when done.

REMOVING ONLY THE NOTE

There is a way to remove only the note and not the highlight:

iOS
- Tap on the text you highlighted above.
- Tap on Note.
- Tap on the trash can icon.
- Tap on Delete.

Or you can do the following:

- Tap on the note icon in the right-hand margin.
- Tap on the menu, three dots (...) in the upper right-hand corner.
- Tap on Delete.

Note: The steps above deleted only the note. Your selection is still highlighted.

Android

- Tap on the text you highlighted above.
- Tap on Note.
- Tap on Option Menu.
- Tap on "Delete Note."

Or you can do the following:

- Tap on Note icon to the right of the text.
- Tap on the Pencil icon.
- Tap on Option Menu.
- Tap on "Delete Note."

REMOVING A NOTE AND HIGHLIGHTING

- Place a finger on any word on the screen. This is for an example, so it does not matter which word you choose.
- Tap on Note.
- Type something (a few letters will do).
- Tap on Save.

Now you have a word that is highlighted and a note attached to it.

- Tap on the word.
- Tap on Remove.

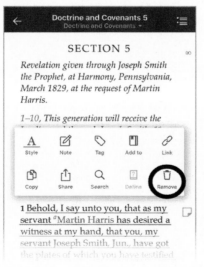

A warning will appear stating everything will be removed.

- Tap on Remove.

REMOVING ONLY THE HIGHLIGHTING

If you do not want the selection you wrote a note on to be highlighted, there is a way to remove the highlighting but not the note. First, create a note to experiment with. You will see that it automatically applies the last highlighting style you were using.

iOS
- Tap on the word.
- Tap on Style.
- Tap on the remove highlighting and style icon.
- Tap anywhere on the screen.

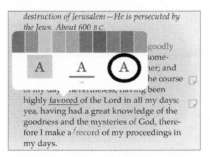

The highlighting is now removed but the Note remains.

Android
- Tap on the word.
- Tap on Style.
- Tap on the remove highlighting and style icon.

- Tap on the check mark.

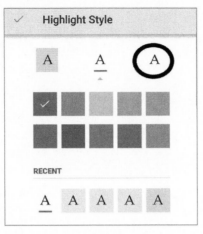

The highlighting is now removed, but the note remains.

COPYING AND PASTING

Perhaps I am stating the obvious, but you can also copy text from another source (for example, a dictionary or something from the web) and paste it into a note.

Copying and pasting with mobile devices is very easy.

- Select text.
- An option menu will appear.
- Tap on Copy.
- Go to the app that you want to paste the content into.
- Place and hold your finger on the screen until a menu appears.
- Tap on Paste.

INTERMEDIATE

Go to 1 Nephi 1:1.

- Select the following: "having seen many afflictions in the course of my days."
- Tap on Notes in the popup menu.
- In the title, type "Afflictions."
- Tap in the body of the note and type the following:

"Even the righteous suffer afflictions. The word comes from the Latin *affigere*, meaning 'infliction of pain or humiliation.'"

- Now bold, italicize, or underline the word *affigere*.
- Tap on Save or the check mark.

TO MODIFY A NOTE

iOS

- Open a note by placing your finger on the selected text attached to the note, and then tap on the note and make your changes. Now tap Save. OR you can do the following:

  » Tap on the note icon in the right margin.
  » Tap on Menu.
  » Tap on Edit Note.
  » Make your changes, and then tap Save.

Android

- Open a note by placing your finger on the selected text attached to the note, and then tap on the note and make your changes. Now tap Save. OR you can do the following:

  » Tap on the Note icon in the right margin.
  » Tap on the edit icon (the pencil).
  » Make your changes, and then save by tapping on the check mark.

REMOVING A NOTE

iOS

- If you open the note by going through the popup menu, then once the note opens, tap on the delete icon.
- If you open the note by tapping on the note icon, tap on Menu / Delete.

Android

- Tap on the note icon, and then tap on Menu / Delete / Delete.

Note: This will also remove any notes, tabs, or links that are attached to this highlight.

REMOVING HIGHLIGHTED
TEXT AND THE NOTE

Tap on the highlighted text, and then tap on Remove.

REMOVE ONLY THE HIGHLIGHTING

Create a note anywhere on the screen.

iOS
- Tap on the highlighted text.
- Tap on Style.
- Tap on the third *A*. This only available if you have a note attached to marked text.

Android
- Tap on the highlighted text.
- Tap on Style.
- Tap on the third *A* at the top.

If you have some texts from another source that you want in a note in the Gospel Library, simply copy and paste. There is a twenty-thousand-character limit to a note. To put this into perspective, the average conference talk is between six thousand and eight thousand characters, so you have plenty of room.

ADVANCED

To create a note, select some text, and then tap on Note. In the note you can bold, italicize, or underline text and create bulleted or numbered lists.

You can delete a note and selected text at the same time or separately. See Intermediate section for instructions.

Day 5: Tags

Organize information by topic for quick retrieval

NOVICE

Study—remember to start and end with prayer.

- In Alma 32:15–16, select "humbleth himself."
- Tap on Tag.
- Type "Humility."
- Tap on Save (for iOS) or the check mark (for Android).

- Select "repenteth."
- Tap on Tag.
- Type "Repentance."
- Tap on Save (for iOS) or the check mark (for Android).

- Select "endureth to the end."
- Tap on Tag.
- Type "Enduring."
- Tap on Save (for iOS) or the check mark (for Android).

- Go to 2 Nephi 31:15.
- Select the entire verse.
- Tap on Tag.
- Tap on "Endure" in the list below.

Once you create a tag, you do not need to type the whole name of the tag again. Just type the first few letters and the tag will appear in the list below the "Add tag" field.

If it does not appear, then it means you have not created that tag yet, or it could mean that you misspelled the tag in the past. Not having to retype a tag is very helpful once you have created, over the years, hundreds of tags.

Note: You can have more than one tag per selected text. Sometimes I have added four or five.

$$\bullet \bullet$$

GOING DEEPER

TAGS ARE INDEXING IN THE DIGITAL AGE

Indexing in the digital age is called a hashtag.

Hashtags were first introduced on Twitter and are now found on other social media sites, like Facebook and Instagram, and are also used in various apps, like the Gospel Library.

For social media, a hashtag consists of the # symbol followed by a single word (e.g., #recipes). To use a phrase as a hashtag, the words must be combined into one word, containing no spaces (e.g., #iloveapplecherryrecipes).

The Gospel Library uses hashtags but has shortened the word to "tags" and made them easier to use. The Gospel Library does not require the hashtag symbol (#), and you can use spaces, commas, parentheses, hyphens, and so on to separate words. For example, I can create a tag called "Feeding the Poor" (instead of having to type #feedingthepoor) or perhaps "Baptism (infant)."

When you create a tag, you are building a personal retrieval system, an indexing system. Tags are not only for use in the scriptures but for anything in the Gospel Library that can be marked. For example, the tag "Faith" could have snippets from a Church magazine, general conference talk, Sunday School manual, and even a video.

> Note: When creating a tag, capitalization is not required. For example, you could use "faith," FAITH," or Faith. With my OCD tendencies, I must have it capitalized.

MULTIPLE-WORD TAGS

- Go to Matthew 21:14.
- Select "he healed them."
- Tap on Tag.
- Type "Character of Christ."
- Tap on the return key on the keyboard.
- Tap on Save (or iOS) or the check mark (for Android).

WHERE TO FIND YOUR TAGS

- Go to the Library.
- Tap on the Notes collection.
- Tap on Tags.

There you will see the Tags that you have created.

SORTING THE TAGS

Tags can be sorted by most recent, name, or count. The most recent sort is great for finding the tags that you have most recently been working with. Of course, sorting by name simply lists the tags in alphabetical order. Sorting by count may appear to be an odd sort, but I like it. From time to time, I sort by count because it helps me to see what I have been focusing on or find the most interesting. To the right is a screenshot of my tags sorted by count.

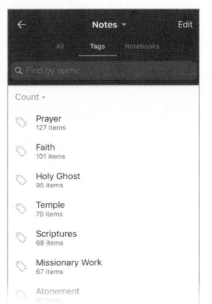

iOS

- To sort, tap in the upper left-hand corner.
- Tap on one of the three choices.

Android

- To sort, tap on the three horizontal lines in the search field.
- Tap on one of the three choices.

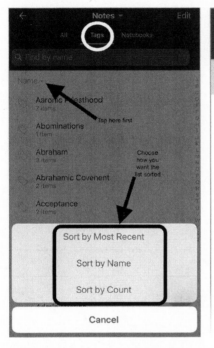

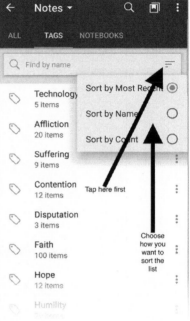

RENAMING TAGS

Correcting a misspelling or changing the name of a tag is simple.

iOS

While in the list of tags

- Tap on edit in the upper right-hand corner.
- Tap on the tag you want to correct.
- Make the correction.
- Tap on Save.

Android

While in the list of tags

- Tap the option menu to the right of the name of the tag.
- Tap on Rename.
- Make the correction.
- Tap on OK.

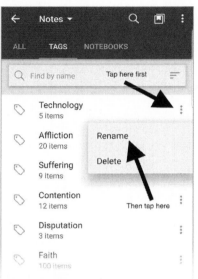

Note: A new addition to the Notes collection is the "All" function. Note that across the top is the word "All." This lists all your tags, notes, links, and highlights/underlining. From this list you can add an item from the list to a notebook or edit and delete an item. The items are listed by date with the most recent date at the top. Tap the option menu for the following options: Edit Note, Duplicate (iOS only), Add to Notebook, Share, or Delete. Tap on a scripture reference to add or delete tags or to edit the marking.

INTERMEDIATE

To add a tag to the following

iOS

- Select some text.
- Tap on Tag.
- Create a tag.
- Tap on Save, OR tap on the return key to add another tag.

Android

- Select some text.
- Tap on Tag.
- Create a tag.
- Tap on the check mark. OR tap on Next to add another tag.

If you have a long list of tags, then do not be so quick to type the full name of the tag you are creating. Type only the first two or three characters. There could be a possibility that you have already created it. If so, it will appear as you type, and then you just need to tap on the tag in the list.

You can have several tags for each selected text.

You can find the list of tags in Library / Notes / Tags. From there you can edit them.

You can also sort them. See Sorting Tags above.

See Advanced section for merging two tags.

ADVANCED

Review Intermediate section if needed.

MERGING TWO TAGS

There is no merging function, but there is a work-around.

Suppose I have two tags: **Administration** and *Aministration*. The latter is spelled wrong. Here is how to solve the problem:

iOS

Tap on the tag *Aministration*. This will open a list of everything you tagged with *Aministration*. Tap on the reference in the first quote. Tap on the note icon to the right of the marked text, and then tap on the *X* in *Aministration* to delete it. Tap on the plus sign, and begin typing **Administration**. A list will show up in the list below. Tap on **Administration**, and then Save. Tap on the scripture.

Tap on the back arrow in the upper left-hand corner to go back to your tag list. Repeat the above steps until the list is empty in *Aministration*, and then delete *Aministration*.

Android

Tap on *Aministration*. This will open a list of everything you tagged with that tag. Tap on the reference in the first quote. Tap on the tag icon to the right of the marked text, then tap on the plus sign. Tap on Cancel Item for *Aministration*, and then add the correct tag and tap on the check mark to save.

Tap on the back arrow in the upper left-hand corner to go back to your tag list. Repeat the above steps until the list is empty in *Aministration*. Then delete that tag.

Day 6: Links

Create a connection between common content

CREATING A LINK

One of the great tools in the Gospel Library is the ability to create your own links. And, even better, it creates a link in both directions. When I create a link from A to B, the link function also creates a back link from B to A.

You do not need to be in the scriptures to create a link. You can create a link between any content that has text. For example, you can create a link between one paragraph in a magazine and a paragraph in a manual, or a sentence in a talk and a scripture. The only rule is that you have to link content that has text.

So what about photos and videos? They can also be linked because each of the photos and videos has a title, so link to the title.

$$\boxed{7\ MINUTES}$$

NOVICE

Study—remember to start and end with prayer.

- Go to Matthew 5:48.
- Read and ponder the verse.
- Select verse 48.
- Tap on Link.
- Tap the cancel icon if needed to clear the search field.
- Type in the search field "n1248."

- Scroll down if needed to find 3 Nephi 12:48.
- Tap on the link icon.
- Do not tap on Save (for iOS) or the check mark (for Android), because you are going to add John 17:23 next.

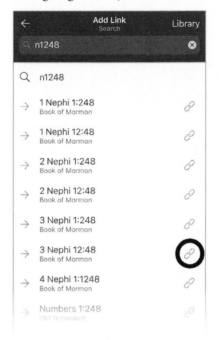

For iOS, notice that at the bottom of the screen you can also go to Multi-screens or Bookmarks to locate content you want to link to.

Now create a link to John 17:23.

- Tap the cancel icon to clear the search field.
- Type in the search field "j1723."

- Scroll down if needed to find John 17:23.

Stop at this point, and notice you always have two options. You can tap on the link icon to automatically create the link as you did with 3 Nephi 12:48, or you can tap on the reference to go to John 17:23 and add additional verses.

Now you are going to create a link to John 17:23 and 24.

- Tap on the reference to John 17:23.
- Scroll down if needed to verse 23.
- Tap on verses 23 and 24 to select them.

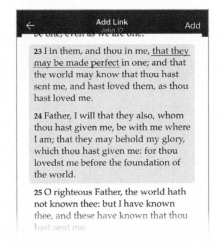

- Tap on Add (for iOS) or the check mark (for Android).

Notice the link is to John 17:23–24. The verses do not need to be consecutive. You could have tapped on verse 23, 25, and 26. Or you could have decided to start in verse 21 and include 22, 23, and 26.

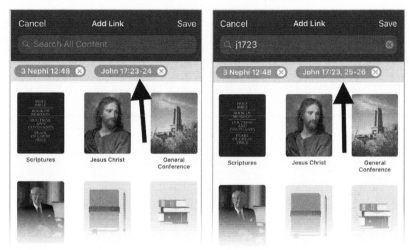

- Tap on Save (for iOS) or the check mark (for Android).

iOS

- Tap on the related content icon and scroll down if needed to see the three links you created.

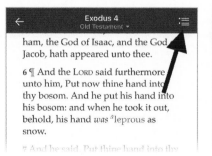

Android

- Tap on the option menu icon.
- Tap on Related Content.

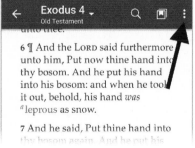

- Read each verse and ponder. Write your feelings or comments about the word "perfect" in a note.

· ·

$\boxed{\textit{GOING DEEPER}}$

DELETING A LINK

To delete a link

iOS

- Tap on the link icon to the right of the verse.
- Tap on the link icon in the reference.
- Tap on the *X* to the right of the link.

Note: If you also have a note attached to the same verse, the link icon will not be in the right margin. You will find it in the note. Tap on the note icon, and then scroll down to the bottom of the note.

iOS

- Tap on the *X* to the right of the link.

Android

- Tap the link icon to the right of the verse.
- Tap on the link icon in the reference.
- Tap on the *X* to the right of the link.
- Tap on the check mark.

Note: If you also have a note attached to the same verse, the link icon will not be in the right margin. You will find it in the note. Tap on the note icon, and then scroll down to the bottom of the note.

INTERMEDIATE

CREATING A LINK

You are going to create to links to Matthew 5:48, 3 Nephi 12:48, and John 17:23.

- Select verse 48 in Matthew 5.
- Tap on Link.
- Type in the search field "n1248."

- Scroll down if needed to find 3 Nephi 12:48. Tap on the reference.
- Tap on the verse 3 Nephi 12:48, and then tap on Add.
- Repeat the process for the other verses.
- Save when completed.

Note: While creating the links, you can choose more than one verse. Simply tap on the verses you want to include in the link. They do not need to be consecutive. You can also create several links at the same time (for example, 3 Nephi 12:48 and John 17:23).

Open the related content and scroll toward the bottom if needed, and there you can see the links you created.

DELETE HIGHLIGHTING AND LINKS

- Tap on verse 48 of Matthew 5.
- Tap on Remove.

ADVANCED

You are going to create links to Matthew 5:48, 3 Nephi 12:48, and John 17:23. You can create them one at time, but you can also do all three at the same time.

- Select Matthew 5:48.
- Create a link to 3 Nephi 12:48 and John 17:23.

You can delete the highlighting and link(s) all at once. Tap on the selected text, and then tap on Remove.

To delete links one at a time without deleting the highlighting, tap on the link icon to the right of the verse, tap on the link icon in the reference, and then cancel the link.

If there is a note also attached to the selected text, then the link icon will be found in the note.

Day 7: Related Content

Locate your notes, tags, and links and the footnotes
of the latest LDS edition of the scriptures

HISTORY

In 1979, The Church of Jesus Christ of Latter-day Saints published the first LDS edition of the scriptures, and among others features extensive footnotes were included to aid in studying the scriptures. The footnotes included cross-references. Further clarification was provided where needed using the codes below.

- HEB & GK—providing alternate Hebrew & Greek translations
- TG—denoting further information in the Topical Guide
- JST—providing references to the Joseph Smith Translation
- IE—helping with idiomatic phrases
- OR—providing clarification on a word or phrase

The Gospel Library has taken all the footnotes from the 1979 edition and added some serious muscle. You can add tags, notes, and links of your own, and—what is really cool—all of the references from the 1979 edition are now links. Tap on a link, and the verse appears without you having to leave the page you are on. In the Gospel Library, footnotes are located in the related content.

7 MINUTES

NOVICE, INTERMEDIATE, ADVANCED

Study—remember to start and end with prayer.

- Go to Exodus 4.
- Read the heading to get a summary of the chapter.
- Read verse 7.
- Look at the word "plucked."

The word is colored and has a superscript "a" preceding it. A word that is colored indicates that there is information about that word in the related content, and the "a" provides the location in the related content.

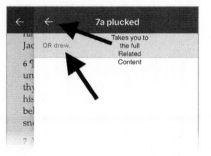

- Tap on the word "plucked."

Now the related content opens the footnote 7a specifically and provides clarification on the word "plucked."

To close

iOS

- Tap on the back arrow, or tap anywhere on the screen other than the related content.

Android

- Tap on the X, or tap anywhere on the screen other than the related content.

- In verse 7, find the phrase "turned again as."

Notice it has a superscript "b."

- Tap on the phrase.

Again, the related content opens the Footnote 7b specifically and explains in Hebrew that it means "restored like." Now close it as before.

- In verse 9, tap on "the river."
- Note the meaning of the "the river" is the Nile.
- Close the related content.
- In verse 9, tap on "blood."
- Now you have the link to another related verse without having to actually turn to that verse.
- If you want to read the verse in context, tap on the scripture reference Exodus 7:19.
- When done, tap on the back arrow to return to Exodus 4.

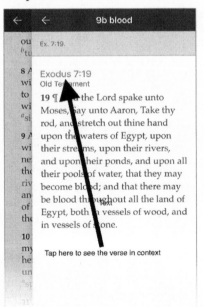

- Close the related content.

OPENING THE RELATED CONTENT

To see the full list of footnotes, open the related content.

iOS

- Tap on the related content icon.

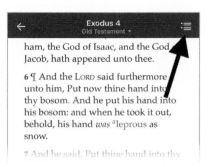

Android

- Tap on the option menu.
- Tap on Related Content.

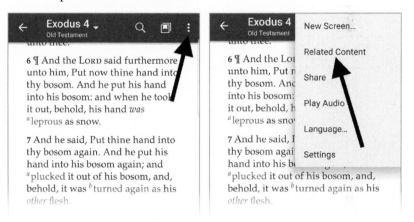

Listed are the footnotes from the printed edition. They have become links. In the digital world, links are almost always in color and often underlined. In black are the clarifications mentioned above.

Day 8: Notebooks

Organize talks, lessons, and ideas, or keep a journal

(*7 MINUTES*)

NOVICE

Study—remember to start and end with prayer.
- Go to the Library.
- Tap on Notes.
- Tap on Notebooks.
- Tap on the plus sign to create a new notebook.

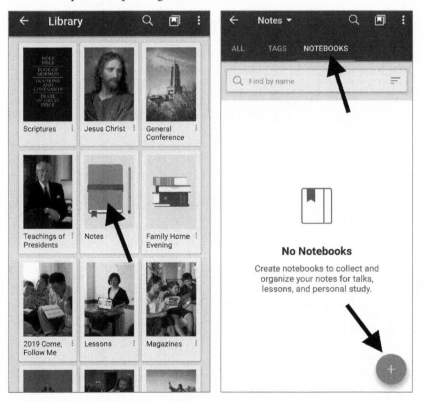

- Type "Baptismal Talk" for the title.
- Tap on Save (for iOS) or the check mark (for Android).

- Find two to four scriptures about baptism. Remember to use the Search function.

iOS	*Android*

iOS

- Select a verse.
- Tap on Add to.
- Tap on the Baptismal Talk notebook.

Android

- Select the verse.
- Tap on Add to.
- Tap on the Baptismal Talk notebook.
- Tap on the check mark.

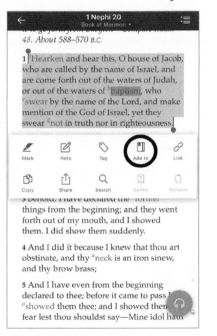

Repeat the above procedure for each verse.

- Using the search function, search for a quote about baptism from a general conference talk.
- Select the text.
- Tap on Add to.

* *

⬡ *GOING DEEPER* ⬡

DELETING A NOTE IN A NOTEBOOK

Go to the Library.

iOS

- Tap on Notes.
- Tap on Notebooks.
- Find the notebook that contains that note you want to delete.
- Tap on Edit.
- Tap on the two arrows in the upper left-hand corner. This will make it easier to see the notes because each note will be reduced to two lines.
- Find the note you want to delete.

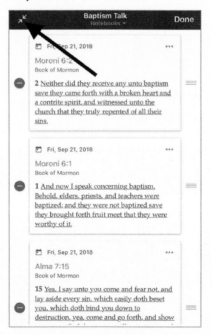

Notice the three dots in the upper right-hand corner of each note.

- Tap on the three dots (option menu), which pulls up a menu of other editing items, including Delete. All of these items will be discussed in another section. Now tap on Cancel.
- Tap on the red circle to the left of the note you want to delete.
- Tap on Delete.
- When finished editing, tap on Done.

There is an easier way to delete.

- While in the notebook, swipe the note you want to delete to the left.

Android

- Tap on Notes.
- Tap on Notebooks.
- Tap on the notebook that contains the note you want to delete.
- Tap on the option menu.

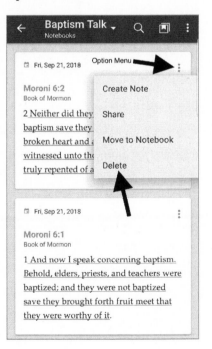

Note: You also have other editing options. We will discuss that in another section.

- Tap on Delete.

INTERMEDIATE

There are three ways that you can add notes to a notebook.

- Selecting text and tapping on Add to in the popup menu.
- From within the notebook, tapping on the plus sign and typing a note.
- Selecting text and tapping on Note, typing a note, and then tapping on Add to Notebook.

You do not need to create a notebook before sending notes to the notebook. You can also create a notebook on the fly.

For study, create a notebook for a sacrament talk on baptism, adding scriptures and personal comments. See the Novice section if you need some ideas.

You can modify or move the notes using the same method for modifying or moving tags.

ADVANCED

Notebooks are found in Library / Notes / Notebooks. They are great for creating a lesson or talk or gathering information on a particular topic. Some people use a notebook for keeping notes during a church meeting. Notebooks can also be created on the fly.

There are two ways to add a note to a notebook.

- Select the text, and tap on "Add to."

Note: With an Android, you can add to more than one notebook at the same time.

- Select text and tap on Note.
- Add same text to the note and then tap on the notebook icon.

Day 9: Notebooks: Adding Comments

Add personal notes to a notebook

(*7 MINUTES*)

NOVICE

Study—remember to start and end with prayer.

- In the Gospel Library, tap on Notes.
- Tap on Notebooks.
- Tap on the Baptismal Talk notebook.
- Find a scripture, and then read it and think about what you want to say about the scripture.
- Tap on the option menu.
- Tap a Create Note.

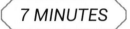

Now add a comment about the scripture.

- Adding a title is optional.
- Type your comment in the body of the note.
- Tap on Save (for iOS) or the check mark (for Android).
- Repeat for each scripture.

You can also create notes in the notebook that are not part of an existing note.

iOS

- While in a notebook, tap on the plus sign.
- Create a title if you feel the need.
- Type your comment in the body of the note.
- Tap on Save.

Android

- While in a notebook, tap on the plus sign.
- Create a title if you feel the need.
- Type your comment in the body of the note.
- Tap on the check mark.

(*GOING DEEPER*)

ORGANIZING THE NOTES IN A NOTEBOOK

Go to the Library.

iOS

- Tap on Notes.
- Tap on Notebooks.
- Tap on the notebook of your choice.
- Tap on Edit.
- Tap on the two arrows in upper left-hand corner. This reduces each note to two lines of text. This will make it easier to move the notes.
- Place your finger on the three horizontal lines to the right of the first note.
- Slide the note down to a new position.
- Lift your finger when you have the note where you want it.

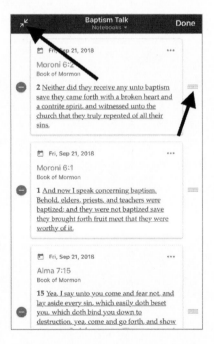

- Continue to place each note in the location you want to move it to by sliding the note up or down.

Android

- Tap on Notes.
- Tap on Notebooks.
- Tap on the notebook of your choice.
- Place you finger on the first note and wait one second.
- You will feel a click, and the note will appear to be slightly raised.
- Slide the note down to a new position.
- Lift your finger when you have your note where you want it.
- Continue to place each note in the location you want to move it to by sliding the note up or down.

Note: If your notes are long, it is difficult to move them. Unlike iOS, you cannot reduce a note to two lines.

ADDING NOTES ATTACHED TO SCRIPTURE TO A NOTEBOOK

Go to Alma 7:14.

- Select verses 14 and 15.
- Tap on Note.
- Type the following:

> "By our willingness to be baptized, we show we are willing to repent and enter into a covenant to keep His commandments."

iOS

- Tap on Add to Notebook in the lower left-hand corner.
- Tap on the Baptismal Talk notebook.
- Tap on Save.

Android

- Tap on the Add to Notebook icon in the upper right-hand corner.
- Tap on the Baptismal Talk notebook.
- Tap on the check mark.

iOS   *Android*

You have just created a note attached to Alma 7:14–15 and at the same time attached it to a notebook.

- Go to the Library.
- Tap on Notes.
- Tap on the Baptismal Talk notebook.

There you can see the note along with the scripture attached to the note.

⦁ ⦁

Days 10, 11, and 12 do not have
scripture study lessons or skill levels.

Day 10: Notebooks vs. Notes

Understand the difference between the
purposes of notebooks and notes

Today there is not a scripture study session. Take your time with this lesson. It is important that you understand the difference between notes located in a notebook and notes attached to content.

There are two tools in the Gospel Library that create confusion: notebooks and notes. The confusion is in the terminology of what a note is. There are two kinds of notes in the Gospel Library: notes created within a notebook and notes created outside of a notebook. The latter is required to be attached to some content. The former is not required.

NOTEBOOK

A notebook stands alone; it does not require interaction within any of the content in the Library. Think of a notebook as an app within an app—the main app being the Gospel Library, and the notebook being an app within the Gospel Library.

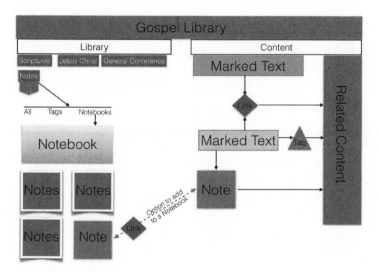

When you create a notebook, you are creating a subject. It is like inserting a title in the binder of a three-ring notebook. Within the notebook are notes related to the subject. These notes are your ideas, impressions, revelations, talks, lessons, and more. Think of these notes as pages. They are created within a notebook and have no relation to other content outside of the notebook.

For example, you could create a notebook of recipes. Each of the pages (notes) would be a separate recipe. While that would not be the best use of a notebook, it helps to bring home the point that the notebook does not need to be attached to content.

In actual practice, you could create a notebook on a lesson or a sacrament talk you are preparing. Each page (note) would be a scripture or quote from a talk from general conference. You might consider having a notebook called "General Conference," and each page could be a quote from a speaker or impressions received during the talk. Perhaps create a notebook for church meetings, and each page (note) would be a different date. These are just a few examples, and I am sure that you will be able to find what will work best for you; let your imagination run wild.

NOTE

A note created outside of a notebook cannot exist alone; it **must be linked to some content**. Think of this kind of note as writing a comment in the margins of the scriptures, a book, or a magazine.

If I were reading Matthew 5:48 in my printed edition of the New Testament and wanted to make a comment that, unlike a similar quote in 3 Nephi 12:48, in Matthew the Savior only mentions the Father, I would write a small note in the margin near verse 48. The comment would have to be very short because of the lack of available space.

However, in the Gospel Library I can select verse 48 and create a note. The size of the note is nearly unlimited and will become part of the related content. The actual character limit is twenty thousand characters. This should be more than enough space for your notes. For example, the average conference talk is between six thousand and eight thousand characters.

Now here is where the confusion begins. I can also link that same note, which is tied to content, to a notebook. Using the above example, I would link the note to a notebook titled "Perfection."

In summary, notebooks and the notes (pages) created in the notebook are independent of other content. Notes created outside of a notebook are linked to specific content and can also be linked to a notebook.

Day 11: Define

Find a definition of a word.

iOS

- Select a word.
- Tap on Define.
- A definition appears.

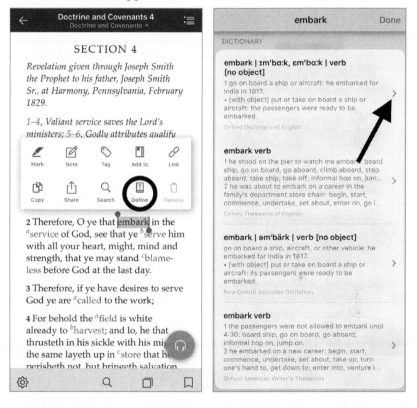

Before you read the definition, let's take a tour. Scroll down the screen. There will be other bits of information related to the word, such as movies, websites, and so on. Your list might be very short or long or in the middle. It depends on how you have Siri set up, which is beyond the scope of this book.

Scroll all the way to the bottom, and you will see Manage Dictionaries. Tap on that to see the options that you have in iOS settings. Pick the dictionaries you want to use. Below is a screenshot of what I use.

Now let's continue with the definition. Because you are in iOS settings, make sure that you tap on Library, in the very upper left-hand corner. You are now back to your scripture.

iOS

- Select the word you had selected previously.
- Tap on Define.
- Read the definition.
- Tap on the arrow to the right for an extended definition.
- Tap on Done when finished reading.

Note: The iOS system does not allow you to copy the definition so that you could create a note to the word you selected. You either have to remember what you read and type it in a note or scroll down and find the Search Web option below the definition and then tap on Search Web to find definitions on the web that you can copy and paste. I also use third-party dictionaries, which will be discussed later.

Android

- Select a word.
- Tap on Define.
- If this is your first time, you may be asked which browser you want to use.
- Using the browser, Android will supply a definition along with other sites that can help with the word.

Note: You are actually taken out of the Gospel Library to use the browser. To return to the Gospel Library, swipe up from the bottom of the screen to bring up the system navigation bar and then tap on the back arrow or use the app list.

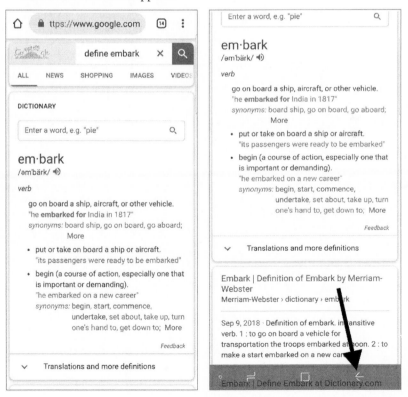

Words have meaning, and not all dictionaries are the same. However, most of the time the definition provided using the Define function will suffice, but there are other times you might want to dig deeper.

One dictionary that I recommend is Webster's 1828 Dictionary. It is available for iOS and Android. The dictionary reflects word usage during the time of Joseph Smith. More information about third-party dictionaries is in Section Four.

Maps

Understand historical events

Maps help us understand distances, topography, and relationships between various locations. They are great in helping us understand events described in the scriptures. For example, the map of "The Division of the 12 Tribes" could be helpful in raising questions about the divisions—Why are the division not equal? Compare that map with the "Physical Map of the Holy Land" to show more detail about the area each tribe received.

USING THE MAPS IN THE GOSPEL LIBRARY

Maps are in the Scriptures collection. You can also use the search function to locate a map.

When you find the map, tap on the map to switch to a zoomable version. Using your thumb and index finger, you can pinch in and out to zoom in and out. The screen resolution on your device will impact the quality of the map. Depending on your screen resolution, zooming in may not be crystal clear. If that occurs, zoom out to the point just before it became not as clear.

MARKING UP A MAP

Find the map you want, and tap on it. Look at the map in both landscape and portrait mode to decide on which provides the best view. Zoom in, if desired, and then, using your finger, move the map around to get your point of interest in the center of the screen. Take a screen shot of the map, and save the map to photos.

iOS
- For iPhones 8+ and below, press the power button and the home button at the same time.
- For iPhones X and higher, press the power button and the volume up button at the same time.

Android
- Press the power button and the volume down button at the same time. There are many different models using the Android

operating system (for example, Samsung, LG, OnePlus, and Moto). If your phone doesn't take a screenshot using the above instruction, then either contact your service provider or search Google for information.

Marking a map with circles, arrows, and so on can be helpful in a classroom setting. This works better on tablets than on mobile phones because of the larger screen. As stated above, this can be a great tool, but you need to play with marking up a map before using it in the classroom.

iOS	*Android*
• After you take a screenshot, it will appear in the lower left-hand corner. Tap on it, and you will see the following:	• After you take a screenshot, it will appear in the lower right-hand corner. Tap on it, and you will see the following:

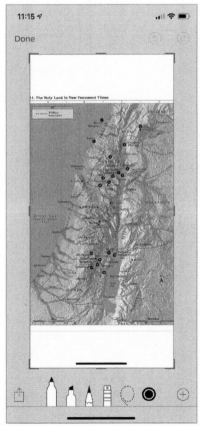 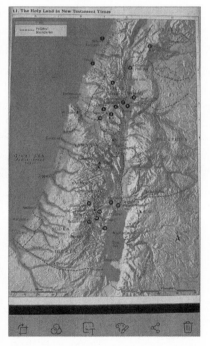

Once you have taken a screenshot, play with the editing tools at the bottom and see what you can do. If you need additional help in marking the photos, go to your friend Google for more information.

USING GOOGLE MAPS

While Google Maps will not have the kind of maps shown in the Gospel Library, it can produce some very fun and interesting maps to help with class discussions. I am going to use the story of Mary and Joseph traveling to Bethlehem as an example.

First, make sure that you have downloaded Google Maps.

- Open Google Maps.
- In the the search field, type "nazareth to bethlehem" (capitalization is not necessary).

You now have the three possible routes taken by Mary and Joseph.

- Tap on the walk icon to show how long it would take to travel each route.

- Tap on the screen to see just the map.

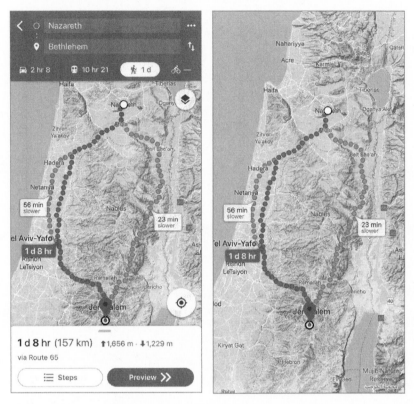

- Take a screenshot.

Note that I said *possible routes*. The routes in the Middle East have not changed a lot over the many centuries and most likely they took one of the routes shown, but that is not the point of creating this map. It is to give the class an idea of how far they had to travel and the terrain they encountered.

Tap on the icon in the upper right-hand corner. Now you can choose between a default, satellite or terrain map.

In a teaching situation, I would choose the terrain map and then ask some of the questions below:

- "Which route do you think Mary and Joseph took? Why?
- "Which route would you prefer to take?"
- "The map is assuming that you are walking a nice, paved road and not the dirt roads of the past. Would this make a difference in comfort and the amount of time it would take to travel the route?"
- "In the time of Mary and Joseph, they didn't have walking shoes. How would that make a difference in travel?
- "We see pictures of Mary traveling on a donkey with Joseph leading the animal. The scriptures say nothing of her using a animal. Do you think a donkey was provided? If not, how would that impact the travel time?"
- "We do not know how far along in her pregnancy Mary was when she arrived in Bethlehem. How would that have impacted the travel time?"
- "Do you think that Mary and Joseph traveled alone?"

Organizing Your Studies

This set of tools helps you organize your studies.

Day 12: Bookmarks

Resume where you left off reading or studying content

> **7 MINUTES**

NOVICE

Study—remember to start and end with prayer.

- Go to 1 Nephi 1.
- Read and ponder the first chapter for about six minutes.
- Select text and create tags and notes as needed.

When done, do the following:

iOS

- Tap on Bookmark.
- Tap on the plus sign.
- Tap on Done in the keyboard.
- Touch the bookmark ribbon, and drag it to the verse you want to start on the next time you study.

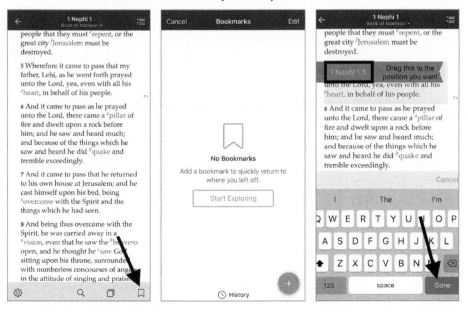

Android

- Make sure that verse you want to start on the next time you study is at the top of the screen.
- Tap on the bookmark icon at the top of the screen.
- Tap on Bookmarks.
- Tap on the plus sign.
- Tap on Add.

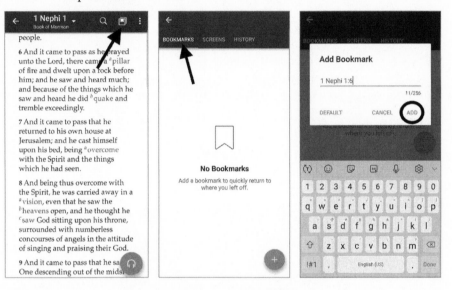

RENAME A BOOKMARK

iOS

- Tap on the bookmark icon.
- Tap on Edit.
- Tap on the bookmark you just created.
- Tap on the cancel icon (the *X* on the right).
- Type "Personal Study."
- Tap on Done or Save.

Android

- Tap on the bookmark icon.
- Tap on Bookmarks if needed.
- Tap on the menu icon of the bookmark you just created.
- Tap on Rename.
- Select the title.

- Tap on the delete key on the keyboard.
- Type "Personal Study."
- Tap on OK.

Now your bookmark is labeled "Personal Study," and the subtitle is the chapter and verse where the bookmark is located.

UPDATE A BOOKMARK

iOS

- Tap on the bookmark icon.
- Tap on the reset icon.
- Place your finger on the bookmark ribbon.
- If needed, drag the ribbon to the verse where you stopped reading.

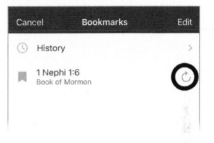

Note: The bookmark can only be placed at the beginning of a paragraph. If you place it in the middle of the paragraph, it will move to the start of the paragraph.

Android

- Scroll up on the page so the verse you want to start on the next time you study is at or near the top of the screen.
- Tap on the Bookmark icon.
- Tap on the menu icon to the right of the bookmark.
- Tap on Update.

Note: Bookmarks are placed at the beginning of the paragraph nearest the top of the screen, so make sure the verse you want is at the top.

DELETE A BOOKMARK

iOS

- Open bookmarks, and place your finger on the right edge of the bookmark.
- Slide your finger all the way to the left of the screen.

Android

- Tap on the bookmark icon.
- Tap on the option menu.
- Tap on Delete.

Or

- Tap on Edit.
- Tap on the red circle to the left of the name.
- Tap on Delete.

· ·

GOING DEEPER

CREATING A LABEL WHEN CREATING A BOOKMARK

iOS

- Tap on Bookmark / plus sign.
- Start typing the title.
- Tap on Done in the keyboard.

Android

- Tap on the bookmark icon at the top of the screen.
- Tap on Bookmarks. (Make sure at the top of the screen Bookmarks is highlighted. If not, tap on Bookmarks.)
- Tap on the plus sign.
- Delete the current title.
- Type the new title.
- Tap on Add.

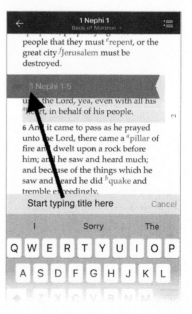

REPOSITIONING BOOKMARKS

After you have several bookmarks, you may want to change the order of the list. I like to put the ones that I use most often at the top.

iOS

- Tap on the bookmark icon.
- Tap on Edit.
- Place your finger on the three horizontal lines in the right-hand margin of one of the bookmarks.
- Slide the bookmark to the location of your choice.
- Release your finger.

Android

- Tap on the bookmark icon.
- Place your finger on one of the bookmarks.
- Wait until the bookmark appears to lift off the screen a little.
- Slide the bookmark to the location of your choice.
- Release your finger.

INTERMEDIATE

iOS

To create a bookmark, tap on the bookmark icon / plus sign / Done.

While in bookmarks, tap on Edit to rearrange, delete, or rename the bookmarks. To rename, tap on the name of the bookmark you want to rename. You can also delete a bookmark by tapping on the bookmark icon and swiping the bookmark you want to delete to the left.

Android

To create a bookmark, tap on bookmark icon / Bookmarks / plus sign / Add. To rename, update, or delete a bookmark, tap on the menu to the right of the bookmark.

ADVANCED

To create, relocate, or edit a bookmark, tap on the bookmark icon.

iOS

- Tap on the bookmark ribbon while in content, and then drag the bookmark to a new location.

Android

- Make sure the content you want to bookmark is at the very top of the screen before creating or updating. There is no way to adjust the location.

Day 13: Personal Collections

Organize content

7 MINUTES

NOVICE

This chapter does not contain a study lesson

CREATE A NEW PERSONAL COLLECTION FOR FAMILY HOME EVENING

iOS

- While in the Library, tap on Edit.
- Tap on the plus sign.
- Type "Family Home Evening."
- Tap on Save.

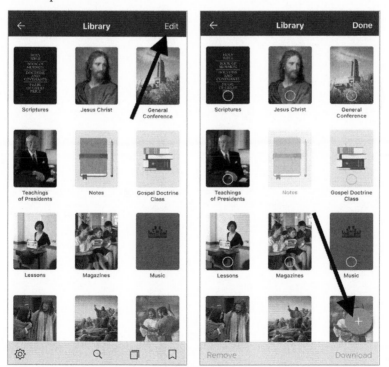

Android

- Tap on the option menu.
- Tap on Custom Collections.
- Tap on the plus sign.
- Type "Family Home Evening."
- Tap on Add.

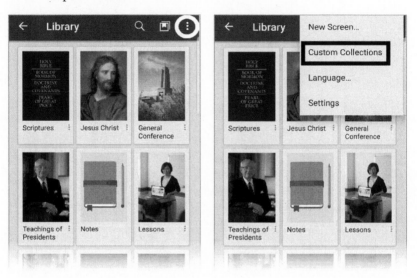

ADDING CONTENT TO
THE NEW COLLECTION

iOS

- Go to the Individuals and Families collection.
- Touch and hold your finger on "The Family: A Proclamation."
- Tap on Add to.
- Tap on Family Home Evening.

- Stay in the Individuals and Families collection.
- Touch and hold your finger on Family Home Evening Resource.
- Tap on Add to.
- Tap on Family Home Evening.

Android

- Go to the Individuals and Families collection.
- Tap on the options menu on "The Family: A Proclamation."
- Tap on Add to.
- Tap on Family Home Evening.

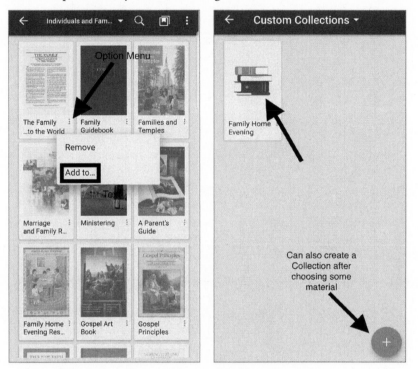

- Stay in the Individuals and Families collection.
- Tap on the options menu on Family Home Evening Resource.
- Tap on Add to.
- Tap on Family Home Evening.

Follow the same procedure to add *True to the Faith*.

Go the Library, and tap on your Family Home Evening collection. You will see the three items that you added.

Note: For both iOS and Android, if what you are adding has not been downloaded, you will have a choice to download or Add to. I suggest you skip the download and tap on Add to. If you download first, then you will have to touch and hold a second time to Add to. By doing an Add to first, the content will be added to your collection, and then when you go to your personal collection and tap on the content, it will automatically download.

GOING DEEPER

DELETING A COLLECTION

In the Library, do the following:

iOS
- Tap on Edit.
- Tap on the Family Home Evening collection.
- Tap on Remove.
- Tap on Remove again.

Android
- Tap on the option menu in the Library.
- Tap on Custom Collections.
- Tap on the option menu of the collection.
- Tap on Delete.
- Tap on Delete again.

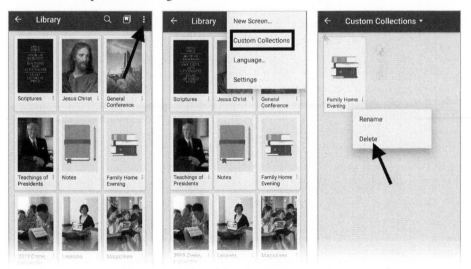

DELETING CONTENT FROM A COLLECTION

iOS

- Open the collection.
- Place your finger on the content you want to remove, and wait for a menu to open.
- Tap on Remove.

Android

- Open the collection.
- Tap on the option menu of the content you want to remove.
- Tap on Remove from Collection.

Now create a collection for your personal needs.

If you are a teacher, create one for your class. If you are the ward mission leader, create a collection called "Ward Mission." If you are a Relief Society president or serve in the presidency, create one called "Relief Society" and add content that you use often. If you are serving as a bishop, create a collection called "Bishop" and add items that you use often with the youth. Also add Handbooks 1 and 2.

Now let your imagination run wild; be creative. If you decide you do not like it or in the future do not need it, delete it.

Note: Deleting from your personal collection does not delete the content from the Library.

INTERMEDIATE

iOS

- In the Library, tap on Edit / plus sign.
- Type a name for your collection.
- Go to any other collection, and find content you want to add.
- Long press on the content you want to add.

Android

- Tap on the menu / Custom Collections.
- Type a name for your collection.
- Go to any other collection, and find content you want to add.
- Tap on the content menu / Add to.

ADVANCED

iOS

- In the Library, tap on Edit / plus sign. Also try a long press on the collection to see other options.
- Go to whatever content you want to add, and then do a long press.

Android

- Tap on the menu in the top right corner.
- Go to the content you want to add, and tap on the content menu.

Multi-screens

Move quickly about content for a lesson or to study

7 MINUTES

NOVICE

CREATING SCREENS

Create several screens in preparation for a hypothetical Gospel Doctrine class on the Old Testament.

- Tap on Lessons.
- Tap on Sunday School.
- Tap on Old Testament: Gospel Doctrine. If it has not been downloaded, you will have to tap again to open it.
- Tap on Lesson 1.

Add the lesson to the multi-screen.

iOS
- Tap on the multi-screen icon.
- Tap on the plus sign.

Purpose

To help class members understand that (1) we are children of God, (2) we can resist Satan's temptations, and (3) God's work and glory is to bring to pass our immortality and eternal life.

Preparation

1. Prayerfully study the following scriptures from the Pearl of Great Price:

Android
- Tap on the bookmark icon.
- Tap on Screens.
- Tap on the plus sign.

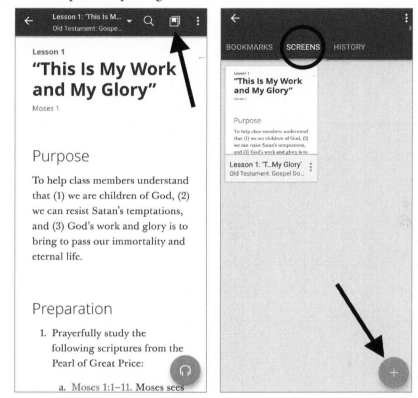

Now, while engaged in prayer and reading the lesson you are preparing to teach, you get the impression that it would help the class to have a review of the Old Testament before discussing the scriptures in the lesson.

After some thought and research, you are led to a great summary in the seminary lesson material on the Old Testament.

- Go to the Library.
- Tap on Seminaries and Institutes.
- Tap on Seminary.
- Tap on Old Testament Study Guide for Home-Study Seminary Students.
- Tap on Welcome to the Old Testament.
- Add to the multi-screen.

iOS
- Tap on the multi-screen icon.
- Tap on the plus sign.

Android
- Tap on the bookmark icon.
- Tap on Screens.
- Tap on the plus sign.

Upon further preparation, you feel that a map of the Middle East during the time of the Old Testament would also be helpful to the class members.

- Go the Library.
- Tap on Scriptures.
- Tap on Bible Maps.
- Tap on 9. The World of the Old Testament.
- Add the map to the multi-screen.

iOS
- Tap on the multi-screen icon.
- Tap on the plus sign.

Android
- Tap on the bookmark icon.
- Tap Screens.
- Tap on the plus sign.

You now have three screens. Tap the multi-screen icon, and tap on any one of the screens to move about the content.

• •

GOING DEEPER

REPOSITIONING SCREENS

iOS
- Tap on the multi-screen icon.
- Tap on Edit.
- Place your finger on the three horizontal lines of one of the screens.
- Slide the screen to the location of your choice.
- Release your finger.

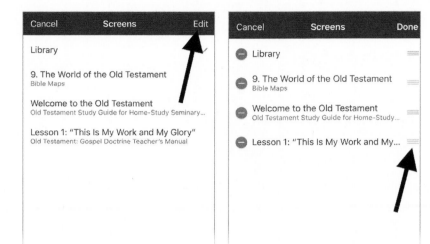

Android

- Tap on the Bookmark icon.
- Tap on Screens.
- Place your finger on one of the screens.
- When you feel a slight vibration, slide the screen to the location of your choice.
- Release your finger.

DELETING SCREENS

iOS

- Tap on the multi-screen icon, and place your finger on the right edge of one of the screens.
- Slide your finger all the way to the left side.

  Or

- Tap on Edit.
- Tap on the red circle to the left of the name.
- Tap on Delete.

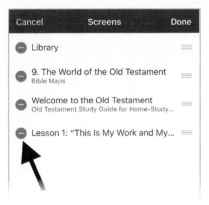

Android

- Tap on the bookmark icon.
- Tap on Screens.
- Tap on the option menu.
- Tap on Delete.

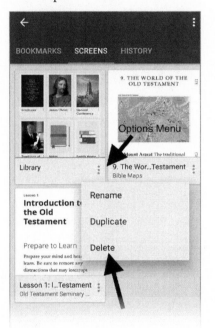

Note: In the option menu, you will also see Rename and Duplicate.

There is often confusion regarding screens and bookmarks. The question I often get is "Should I use bookmarks or screens to move about the Library?" It depends on what you want to accomplish.

Bookmarks are specific and fixed, and Screens are general and fluid.

Bookmarks point to a specific verse or paragraph and will return you to that specific point each time even if you should scroll down or swipe left or right.

Screens point to a specific screen, providing no indication of which verse or paragraph you wish to focus on. This is why the title of a Screen does not contain a verse number. If you were to scroll down or swipe left or right, then the next time you return to that Screen, you would be at the screen you last viewed.

EXAMPLES

If you bookmark 1 Nephi 3:7 and then scroll down to the end of the chapter or swipe right to chapter 4, the next time you tap on the Bookmark for 1 Nephi 3:7, it will return to 1 Nephi 3:7.

If you had created a Screen that showed 1 Nephi 3:7 and then you scrolled down to the end of the chapter, then the next time you tap on the Screen for 1 Nephi 3 (verse numbers are not shown in a Screen title) you would see the last screen you viewed, which was the screen that showed verse 31. Because of this, you need to be careful and remember to return to the original screen. If you had swiped to chapter 4, the title of Screen would have changed to 1 Nephi 4.

I tend to use Bookmarks for studying and Screens for lesson or talks. However, there is no right or wrong way. Just make sure you understand the difference.

INTERMEDIATE

- Tap on Lessons / Sunday School / Old Testament: Gospel Doctrine / Lesson 1

Add the lesson to the multi-screen.

iOS
- Tap on multi-screen / plus sign.

Android
- Tap on Bookmark / Screens / plus sign.

Follow the same steps to add from the Seminaries and Institutes collection.

- Old Testament Study Guide for Home-Study Seminary Students.

Now add from the Scriptures collection.

- Map 9. The World of the Old Testament.

You now have three screens. Tap the multi-screen icon, and then tap on any one of the screens to move to the content.

ADVANCED

iOS has its own icon. For Android the icon is buried in the bookmark icon.

The process is the same for either device.

- Go to your first page, and then go to multi-screen / plus sign.
- Find the second content, and then go to multi-screen / plus sign.
- Continue for each content you want to add.

To reposition, use the same method as with bookmarks.

Editing Your Research

We all make mistakes and sometimes change our minds. One power of the Gospel Library is the ability to edit. This section does not have a study session and is not divided into skill levels.

Day 14: Edit, Delete, Remove, Duplicate, and Copy

Correct errors and make copies

EDITING A NOTE LINKED TO CONTENT

iOS

- Tap on the highlighted content that the note is attached to.
- Tap on Note.
- Make your corrections.
- Tap on Save.

Or

- Tap on the note icon to the right of the highlighted text.
- Tap on the option menu.
- Tap on Edit Note.
- Tap on Save.

Android

- Tap on the highlighted content that the note is attached to.
- Tap on Note.
- Make your corrections.
- Tap on the check mark.

Or

- Tap on the note icon to the right of the highlighted text.
- Tap on the pencil icon.
- Tap on Edit Note.
- Tap on the check mark.

EDITING NOTES IN A NOTEBOOK

To edit a note in the notebook, tap on options menu / Edit Note. This only works with notes you have *created* in the notebook. Notes that are linked to content have to be edited at their source as shown above. To get to the source, tap on the note's title.

DELETE

If you need to remove a note, you can find Delete in the options menu of the note.

Suppose you have a note, tag, and link attached to some content, and you want to remove only one of them without removing the highlighted content. The following is the quickest way.

iOS
- Note—Tap on the note icon to the right of the marked text, and then tap on option menu / Delete.
- Tag—Tap on the note icon, and then tap on Cancel (the x).
- Link—Tap on the note icon / link icon then tap on Cancel (the x).

Android
- Note—Tap on Note icon to the right of the text. Tap on the Pencil icon. Tap on Option Menu. Tap on "Delete Note."
- Tag—Tap on Note icon to the right of the text. Tap on the Pencil icon. Tap on the Tag icon. Tap on Cancel (the x)
- Link—Tap on Note icon to the right of the text. Tap on the Pencil icon. Tap on the Link icon. Tap on Cancel (the x)

REMOVE

To remove highlighting or any note, tag, or link attached to the content, do the following:

iOS
- Tap on the highlighted content.
- Tap on Remove.

You will receive a warning that this action will remove everything connected to the content.

- Tap on Remove.

Android
- Tap on the highlighted content.
- Tap on Delete.

You will receive a warning that this action will remove everything connected to the content.

- Tap on Delete.

FOR iOS AND ANDROID

To remove the highlighting without removing any attachments, do the following:

iOS
- Tap on the selected content.
- Tap on Style.
- Tap on the *A* at the end of the row. (This is ghosted if there is no marked content.)

Android
- Tap on the selected content.
- Tap on Style.
- Tap on the *A* at the end of the top row.

DUPLICATE

Duplicating a note works the same way regardless of the kind of note. To copy a note previously created in the related content and paste it in a notebook, do the following while in a note:

iOS
- Tap on options menu / Duplicate.

Android
- Tap on options menu / Add to Notebook.

Note: Instead of calling it Duplicate, Android makes it much clearer by calling the function Move to Notebook.

COPY

To copy the selected text to the systems clipboard in iOS or to the clip tray in Android, do the following:

iOS and Android

- Select text.
- Tap on Copy.

Once you have tapped on Copy, you can then paste content into another application.

SECTION THREE

Putting It All Together

SOME BACKGROUND

In this section I am going to share with you how I use the Gospel Library during my scripture study. It is kind of like looking over my shoulder as I study.

Some Preparation

THIRD-PARTY APPLICATIONS

There are some free third-party apps that are beneficial to download. They are part of my everyday tools, and I refer to them in the following section. The apps are available for free in the Apple Store or the Play Store. Please download the following.

- Blue Letter Bible (BLB)
- LDS Citation Index
- Terminology or WebWord (dictionary)
- 1828 Webster Dictionary

The above are also available online for those using a desktop or laptop.

- Blue Letter Bible (https://www.blueletterbible.org)
- LDS Citation Index (http://scriptures.byu.edu)
- Dictionary (from any browser, type the word in the search field)
- 1828 Webster Dictionary (http://webstersdictionary1828.com)

Following is a description and some tips on using the apps.

BLUE LETTER BIBLE

The Blue Letter Bible contains Strong's Exhaustive Concordance to the Bible and other English translations and commentaries (though not LDS commentaries). There are other apps that only contain Strong's Concordance, but they require you to purchase the app (or they are free require a subscription for full function of the app). While this app is free, the creators of the app suggest making a donation if you feel that it has been useful.

For those unfamiliar with Strong's Exhaustive Concordance to the Bible, here is a very brief history:

Dr. James Strong (1822–1894) was a professor at Drew Theological Seminary in Madison, New Jersey. Dr. Strong oversaw the exhaustive indexing of the King James Version of the Bible. Each English word is linked to the original Hebrew or Greek text. Strong's Concordance was published just four years before his death. What is amazing is that this was done before the age of computers. The concordance is about four to five inches thick and is of considerable weight. However, it has now been digitalized and can fit in our pocket.

The concordance enables us to study the Hebrew or Greek without having to have knowledge of either language.

The app has plenty of options and tools. It is beyond the scope of this book to explain all aspects of the app. Because the app contains commentaries and has various search options, I am going to explain where to find the concordance.

Tap on the very center of the blue title bar. Tap on NT and then Matthew. Tap on 5, and then scroll down to verse 48. Tap anywhere on verse 48, and then tap on Interlinear/concordance. In the Greek Interlinear section, scroll so you can see the word "perfect." Tap on the Greek word *teleioß* (*telios*), found to the right of the word "perfect."

You are now on the page that shows what the meaning of the word is in Greek. We learn that it does mean "perfect" as we understand the word but also means "brought to its end, finished, complete."

Scroll down further and see how the word is used in context for each verse.

LDS SCRIPTURE CITATION INDEX

The LDS Scripture Citation Index (or Citation Index) was developed by Stephen W. Liddle and Richard C. Galbraith, both from BYU, and is available online at www.scriptures.byu.edu and as an app. They have indexed all of the general conference talks from 1942 to present, as well as the *Journal of Discourses*, Topical Index to the *Journal of Discourses*, and *Scriptural Teachings of the Prophet Joseph Smith.*

You may wonder why the app is recommended when the Gospel Library has conference talks.

First, the Gospel Library only goes back to April 1971 in the conference talks, while the Citation Index goes back to 1942.

Secondly, the Gospel Library does not contain the *Journal of Discourses*, which can be useful at times. The Church official website states, "The *Journal of Discourses* is not an official publication of The Church of Jesus Christ of Latter-day Saints. It is a compilation of sermons and other materials from the early years of the Church, which were transcribed and then published. It included some doctrinal instruction but also practical teaching, some of which is speculative in nature and some of which is only of historical interest."[36]

Thirdly, the Gospel Library does not contain *Scriptural Teachings of the Prophet Joseph Smith.*

And fourthly, the search function in the Citation Index is far more robust because it uses an open-source Lucene search engine. To the right is an example.

Search	Help

Search Terms	Finds Documents ...
angels stand sentinels	Finds documents containing any combination of these words.
+angels +stand +sentinels	Finds documents containing all three words.
-angels +sentinels	Finds documents containing "sentinels" but not "angels".
"angels sentinels"~10	Finds documents where "sentinels" is separated from "angels" by at most 10 words.
"angels who stand"	Finds documents containing the exact phrase "angels who stand".
+Uchtdorf +hope	Finds all talks from President Uchtdorf including the word "hope". Note that this actually finds all documents that include the words "Uchtdorf" and "hope", but often documents containing the word "Uchtdorf" are his talks.
angel*s	Finds documents containing any word starting with "angel" and ending with "s"

Citation Index	Library	Search

---

36. "Journal of Discourses," https://www.lds.org/topics/journal-of-discourses?lang=eng.

Here is a short journey into the beauty of this app.

Open the app, and tap on Citation Index in the lower left-hand corner. Scroll down to the Book of Mormon. You may have to tap on Books in the upper left-hand corner to see all the books.

Citation Index				
2 Tim. [681]	Titus [104]	Philem. [6]	Heb. [1953]	James [935]
1 Peter [928]	2 Peter [649]	1 John [623]	2 John [28]	3 John [24]
Jude [139]	Rev. [3040]			
Book of Mormon				**[18953]**
Title [65]	Intro. [17]	3 Wit. [68]	8 Wit. [35]	1 Nephi [1828]
2 Nephi [3058]	Jacob [588]	Enos [157]	Jarom [23]	Omni [62]
W of M [23]	Mosiah [2211]	Alma [4361]	Hel. [668]	3 Nephi [2848]
4 Nephi [220]	Morm. [540]	Ether [850]	Moroni [1331]	
Doctrine and Covenants				**[27410]**

Notice that 1 Nephi has a number in parentheses, which is the number of times 1 Nephi has been quoted in general conference talks.

Tap on 1 Nephi. Now you have a list of the chapters in 1 Nephi, each with a number in parentheses that represents the number of times the chapter has been quoted.

‹ Books		1 Nephi		
1 [90]	2 [115]	3 [166]	4 [70]	5 [47]
6 [11]	7 [14]	8 [180]	9 [14]	10 [77]
11 [158]	12 [59]	13 [156]	14 [113]	15 [127]
16 [44]	17 [150]	18 [32]	19 [101]	20 [8]
21 [16]	22 [80]			

At the time of this writing, chapter 3 has been quoted the most. Tap on chapter 3 to see a further breakdown of what was quoted. 1 Nephi 3:7 currently has been quoted ninety-five times. Tap on verse 7, and a list of speakers will appear. Tap on a speaker to see the full talk in which the scripture was quoted.

‹ 1 Nephi	**1 Nephi 3**	📖		‹ 1 Ne. 3	**1 Ne. 3:7**	📖
1 Ne. 3:3	[2] ›			**2018–A:63, Henry B. Eyring** Inspired Ministering		
1 Ne. 3:4	›			**2017–A:21, Henry B. Eyring** Gathering the Family of God		
1 Ne. 3:5	[6] ›			**2014–O:73, Henry B. Eyring** Continuing Revelation		
1 Ne. 3:6	›			**2013–A:92, Thomas S. Monson** Obedience Brings Blessings		
1 Ne. 3:6-7	›			**2013–A:124, Elaine S. Dalton** Be Not Moved!		
1 Ne. 3:7 ➡	[95] ›			**2012–A:69, Thomas S. Monson** Willing and Worthy to Serve		
1 Ne. 3:7-8	›			**2010–O:73, Henry B. Eyring** Trust in God, Then Go and Do		
1 Ne. 3:7,15	›			**2009–O:9, Richard G. Scott** To Acquire Spiritual Guidance		
1 Ne. 3:8	[2] ›			**2009–O:101, Michael T. Ringwood** An Easiness and Willingness to Believe		
1 Ne. 3:9	›			**2007–O:54, Walter F. González** Today Is the Time		
1 Ne. 3:13	[4] ›			**2007–A:15, John B. Dickson** Commitment to the Lord		
1 Ne. 3:14	›			**2007–A:95, Charles W. Dahlquist II** Who's on the Lord's Side?		
1 Ne. 3:15	[9] ›			**2006–O:37, Dieter F. Uchtdorf**		

| 🔖 Citation Index | 📚 Library | 🔍 Search | | 🔖 Citation Index | 📚 Library | 🔍 Search |

As mentioned above, the app uses the open-source Lucene search engine. To learn how to use its search capabilities, read the app overview, which shows examples of how to perform various searches.

To locate the overview, tap on Search in the lower right-hand corner, and then tap on Show options in the upper right-hand corner. Scroll down to Help / How to Search.

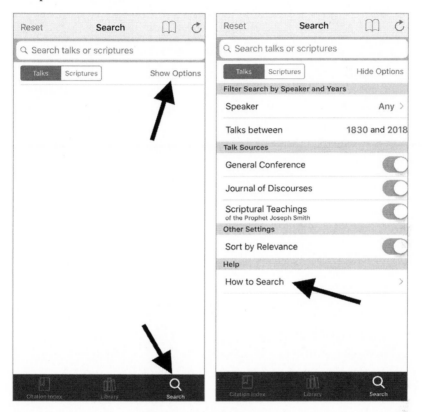

DICTIONARIES

As I used to tell my students in middle school and high school, the dictionary is your best friend. I am not sure that I was ever able to convince them of that, but I hope that you will take it to heart and make sure you have several dictionaries available. Not all dictionaries are the same. Below are four that I recommend.

TERMINOLOGY (iOS)

According to their website, Terminology, "is part dictionary/thesaurus and part research tool" (http://agiletortoise.com/terminology). The app is free.

1828 WEBSTER DICTIONARY (iOS & ANDROID)

It helps to understand how words were used during the time Joseph Smith was translating the Book of Mormon. The app is free, but be careful—there are similar apps that require a fee.

OXFORD ENGLISH DICTIONARY (iOS & ANDROID)

This dictionary goes beyond most other dictionaries and is very helpful, but an app is not available. You can buy a hard copy, but it is expensive and heavy. It is also available on CD, which I would not recommend buying because it is old technology and many of today's laptops and desktop computers do not have CD drives.

The best way to have access to the dictionary is online. Access is free through your local library. If your local library does not have it, check with a regional library.

You do not need to drive to the library. Call them and see if they have it available online. If they do and you have a library card with them, you have free access.

GOSPELINK

This is not an app. It a website that I have used for many years, and I strongly suggest you take a look at it. It is subscription based, but I believe that it is well worth the cost. It is Deseret Book's digital library and contains over 257,000 searchable documents. The cost is $4.99 per month or $49.95 yearly. They offer a thirty-day free trial. Go to http://www.gospelink.com to see everything they have to offer. You will have the opportunity to see how I use Gospelink in my study of the scriptures later in this section.

OTHER RESOURCES

We have been blessed with many knowledgeable men and women who have written books to help in the study of the scriptures.

For example, the *Verse by Verse* series, by D. Kelly Ogden and Andrew C. Skinner, *Searching the Scriptures* by Gene R. Cook, or *Scripture Study* and *The Book of Mormon Made Harder*, both by James E. Faulconer, are all wonderful resources.

By the way, I only purchase hard copies of books if there is no other choice. Instead I purchase digital copies. I do this for two reasons.

First, if I want to take a sentence or paragraph from the book and put it into my Gospel Library notes, I can use the copy and paste function of the device; this is much faster and more accurate than typing it in a note. Always add the name of the resource and the author(s) at the bottom of the note.

Second, if the books are digital, I always have the books with me. I have on my devices hundreds of books, and they are available whenever I need them or have a few moments to read.

HOW TO MOVE BETWEEN APPS

Because you will be switching between several apps, it is important to learn the simple tricks to move among the apps. There are several ways to switch between apps.

iOS

For all iPhones except for the iPhone X, do the following.

- Double press on the Home button.
- Swipe to the right or left to find the app you want.
- Tap on the app to open it.
- Repeat the steps to return to the first app.

For the iPhone X, do the following.

- Swipe up from the bottom to the middle of your screen and hold until you see the app switcher.
- Swipe left or right to find the app that you want to use.
- Tap the app.
- Repeat the steps to return to the first app.

For iOS 9 or an iPhone 6s and up, do the following.

- With your left thumb really close to the left edge of the screen (the thumb is almost half on and half off the screen) press down firmly until you see the screen slides to the right.
- Tap on the second screen. To switch back, do the same procedure.

Android

- Tap on the recent apps icon, and tap on the the app you want to open.

Note: Because of the various models of Android phones and different versions of operating software, if the above does not work, then search Google for help with your particular model.

SECTION FOUR

EXAMPLES FROM MY STUDIES

Doctrine and Covenants 4

My study of D&C 4 was not a onetime event. Initially I spent about a week or longer studying this section. While you can read this chapter in less than seven minutes, it will take longer when following along on your device. So take small sections at a time.

INTRODUCTION

Chapter headings are an important tool in understanding the scriptures and can be marked with all the functions available elsewhere. Notice that I do exactly that in the heading of Doctrine and Covenants 4. I mark the text and add a note as shown below.

After reading this section, I felt that I needed some background information. I found the following information in Gospelink. It hit home to me, and I thought it would make an excellent comment to the introduction.

> This revelation is very short, only seven verses, but it contains sufficient counsel and instruction for a life-time study. No one has yet mastered it. It was not intended as a personal revelation to Joseph Smith, but to be of benefit to all who desire to embark in the service of God. It is a revelation to each member of the Church, especially to all who hold the Priesthood. Perhaps there is no other revelation in all our scriptures that embodies greater instruction pertaining to the manner of qualification of members of the Church for the service of God, and in such condensed form than this revelation. It is as broad, as high and as deep as eternity. No elder of the Church is qualified to teach in the

Church, or carry the message of Salvation to the world, until he has absorbed, in part at least, this heaven-sent instruction.[37]

I copied the quote from the Gospelink site and then returned to D&C 4, highlighted the heading, tapped on Note, pasted the quote into the note, and titled it "Introduction." I then bolded the text that stood out to me. I also showed the source.

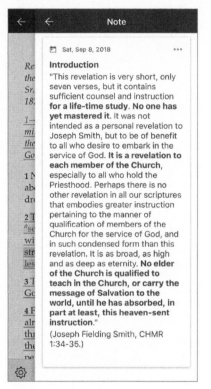

VERSE 1

Now behold, a marvelous work is about to come forth among the children of men.

In the related content, footnotes created by the editors of the LDS Edition of the Scriptures are an invaluable tool and are the first things I look at when reading a verse and want some further understanding.

---

37. Joseph Fielding Smith, CHMR 1:34–35.

I notice there is a footnote for "marvelous" indicating a footnote in the related content, so I tap on the word "marvelous."

Note that all the nine references are on the right of the screen. I scroll down to read each one. Then I go back to the first reference—Isaiah 29:14.

I notice that "marvellous work" is in Isaiah 29:14 in the Old Testament. I love it when a word or phrase in the Book of Mormon, Doctrine and Covenants, or Pearl of Great Price is also found in the Old Testament or New Testament because I can then turn to the original Hebrew or Greek to get a better understanding of how the word was used in other scriptures.

I go to the Blue Letter Bible (BLB) and find Isaiah 29:14. I tap on Interlinear/concordance section and see the word "marvelous." I then tap on the Hebrew word to begin studying the page.

CREATING A NOTE

Finding the information I read helpful, I proceed to copy and paste it into a note in the Gospel Library.

Because I am familiar with Hebrew, sometimes I like to have the Hebrew word in my notes. So I copy and paste it in my note in the Gospel Library. I proceed to do the following:

- Tap on אָלֶף to select it, and then tap on Copy.
- Switch to the Gospel Library.
- In D&C 4:1, select "marvelous work."
- Tap on Note.
- Touch and hold in the body of the note until a menu appears.
- Tap on paste.
- Tap on the space bar.

Note: iOS devices will paste the Hebrew to the left of the screen. Android will paste the Hebrew to the right of the screen, which is correct because Hebrew is read from right to left.

I do not save the note at this point. I then do the following:

- Switch back to the BLB.

- Select and highlight the transliteration *pala*, and then
- Tap on copy.
- Switch back to D&C 4.
- Touch and hold until the menu appears in the note.
- Tap on paste.
- Tap on the return key on the keyboard.

I do not save the note at this point. I then switch back to the BLB:

- Select the section Outline of Biblical Usage starting at "to be marvelous."
- Switch back to the Gospel Library, D&C 4.
- Paste the outline in the note.
- Tap on the return key on the keyboard.
- Add a reference to help me remember where I found the information.
- Tap in the title section.
- Type "marvelous work."
- Tap on Save.

At this point I also copy and paste the above information into Isaiah 29:14.

- Tap on the note icon in the right-hand margin.
- Tap on the option menu icon.
- Tap on Share.
- Tap on Copy.
- Tap on the back arrow.
- Scroll and find the reference to Isaiah 29:14 in the related content.
- Tap on the reference.
- Tap on the reference again—I am now in Isaiah 29:14.
- Select "marvelous work" in verse 14.
- Tap on Note.
- Tap on Paste.
- Add the title.
- Tap on Save.
- Return to D&C 4 by tapping on the back arrow in the upper left-hand corner.

To my note, I also added a definition of "marvellous" from the Old English Dictionary and a quote from Joseph Fielding Smith regarding his definition of the phrase.

Adj
Such as to excite wonder or astonishment (chiefly in a positive sense); wonderful, astonishing, surprising; worthy of admiration. Also having remarkable or extraordinary (and as if supernatural) properties.
OED

President Joseph Fielding Smith defined the phrase and connected it to Isaiah's messianic prophecy that the Lord would "do a marvellous work among this people, even a marvellous work and a wonder" (Isa. 29:14). Moreover, President Smith taught that "this marvelous work is the restoration of the Church and the Gospel with all the power and authority,

Note: The above steps may appear to be complicated, but with practice it will become easier as you continue to create notes in related content.

TIME TO STUDY

The above procedure of creating notes in the related content is one key to scriptural study. From this point on, I will not provide a detailed description of the process as I have done above. So take the time now to study what I demonstrated above. Work through the steps using your device.

Create notes, copy and paste, and switch back and forth between apps. Then, when you feel you have that procedure down, remove your practice notes.

CITATION INDEX

I now open the Citation Index.

- Tap on Citation Index icon in the lower left-hand corner.
- Scroll down to the Doctrine and Covenants.
- Tap on Sections.
- Tap on 4.
- Tap on D&C 4:1–2.
- Begin perusing what the various speakers said about verse 2 in Doctrine and Covenants 4.

I found a comment David O. McKay made about Doctrine and Covenants 4:1–2 and attached it to "service of God" in verse 1 and titled it "Qualifications."

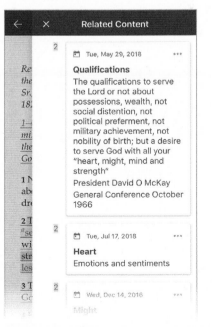

VERSE 2

Therefore, O ye that embark in the service of God, see that ye serve him with all your heart, mind, mind and strength, that ye may stand blameless before God at the last day.

While it may appear that I am nit-picking, I strongly believe *it is not how much we read, but how much we understand that is important.* So I'm going to take the time to make sure I understand what the word "therefore" means. To find the definition, I turn to my best friend, the dictionary. I am first going to use the built-in dictionary in the options menu.

After using the Define tool in the Gospel Library, I opened the app Terminology and found this definition: "Used to introduce a logical conclusion. Synonym – hence, thus, so." I like that definition, and I copied and pasted it into a note attached to the word "therefore."

Now I selected the word "embark" and checked that definition. Tap on the arrow on the right to see more definitions. The definition that I like is the third definition, which states:

Begin (a course of action, especially one that is important or demanding).

The words, "important" and "demanding" have particular interest to me and are why I chose this definition. I used my short-term memory (very short term) and typed the definition into a note attached to "embark."

Next in this verse, I focused on the words "heart, might, mind and strength." I highlighted each of the words in a different color and added a note to each word. The notes that I entered were the following. Your words or definitions may be different and longer (and maybe more insightful).

- Heart: emotions and sentiments
- Might: willpower

- Mind: intellect and reasoning ability, having a mindset of wanting to do His will
- Strength: time and energy

VERSE 3

Therefore, if ye have desires to serve God ye are called to the work;

At this point I stopped and summarized what I had learned. I typed the following in a note connected to the third verse.

Because the Gospel is being restored with all of its "power, authority and keys" I need to be careful and pay attention as I am serving the Lord, I need to understand I am on a course of action that is important and demanding. To help me accomplish that I have been counseled to make sure that my heart, might, mind and strength are all used in that service, I need to be fully involved, otherwise I will not be found blameless before God at the last days.

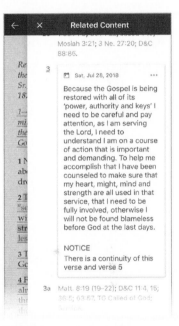

Please note that I use the first person to make it a personal application to me. This note helps me to tie in with the comment from Joseph Fielding Smith and helps me to understand how serious my responsibilities are as I strive to serve the Lord.

I am also following the counsel of Elder Bednar, who suggested that we "write [our] thoughts and feelings" and further explained that "writing about what we think and feel as we study the scriptures helps us to revisit the same spirit that brought the initial insight or revelation and invites even greater understanding than was originally received."[38]

---

38. David A. Bednar, "Understanding the Importance of Scripture Study" (Ricks College devotional, Jan. 6, 1998).

VERSE 4

For behold the field is white already to harvest; and lo, he that thrusteth in his sickle with his might, the same layeth up in store that he perisheth not, but bringeth salvation to his soul;

Being a city boy, I highlighted the word "harvest" and made a note with comments about the word. I entered in the note that "harvest" is a verb, which reminds me it is an action, and then I entered a few synonyms.

Later I found additional information about "the field is white."

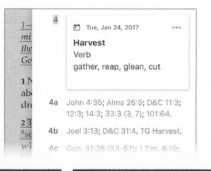

One advantage to using a printed form of the scriptures is the ability to bracket: draw a bracket in the margin to connect two verses and show a relationship between them, or bracket several verses along with a key word.

To overcome that limitation in the Gospel Library, I use color.

While studying D&C 4, I was struck with the relationship or continuity of verses 2 and 4 and the same for verses 3 and 5. Verses 2 and 4 together read as follows:

2. Therefore, O ye that embark in the service of God, see that ye serve him with all your heart, might, mind and strength, that ye may stand blameless before God at the last day.

4. For behold the field is white already to harvest; and lo, he that thrusteth in his sickle with his might, the same layeth up in store that he perisheth not, but bringeth salvation to his soul.

And verses 3 and 5:

3. Therefore, if he have desires to serve God ye are called to the work.

5. And faith, hope, charity and love, with an eye single to the glory of God, qualify him for the work.

I underlined verses 2 and 4 in blue and verses 3 and 5 in red and then added a note to verses 2 and 3. The note in verse 2 states, "Notice the continuity of this verse and verse 4." I decided not to add a title to this note.

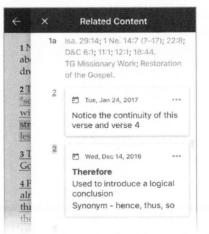

Because I already have a note for verse 3, I added a "NOTICE" to the end of the note, "There is a continuity of this verse and verse 5."

I am not suggesting there is some deep meaning in combining the verses as I did. I understand that others might disagree, and that is okay. I simply found it interesting, and it helps me to better understand what is required of me.

VERSE 5

And faith, hope, charity and love, with an eye single to the glory of God, qualify him for the work.

To this verse I added the tags "Service," "Charity," "Faith," and "Hope."

VERSE 6

Remember faith, virtue, knowledge, temperance, patience, brotherly kindness, godliness, charity, humility, diligence.

I added the tags "Character" and "Qualifications" and then created a link to 2 Peter 1:5–10.

VERSE 7

Ask, and ye shall receive; knock, and it shall be opened unto you. Amen.

This section is normally connected to missionary service and thus often thought of as only applying to missionaries. However, in studying this section I learned from Joseph Fielding Smith that this section "is a revelation to each member of the Church."

So in studying D&C 4, I struggled with the tremendous responsibility that I have and what is required to carry out that responsibility. I wondered how I could possibly meet those qualifications.

After several days of pondering and prayer, I saw verse 7 as the answer to my question.

I selected verse 7 and highlighted it in a color that I have not used in this section and that would stand-out; I chose yellow. Then I added this note: "I need to turn to the Lord for help on how manage my time and serve Him to the fullest of my ability," and added the title "The Answer." Also, I created a "Prayer" tag and created a link to Ether 12:27.

This just begins to touch the surface of what can be done. Notice that I used notes, links, and tags. I copied

from other outside resources. Also, notice that I made use of different colors in underlining and highlighting.

As pointed out by Joseph Fielding Smith, my study of D&C 4 is not complete. As I engage in further study of this section, I will receive, from time to time, additional revelation and record it in my notes, create more tags, form additional links, and so on.

Perhaps it will be discussed in a class and a comment will be made that provides me further understanding of the section, or a comment made in a general conference talk will provide further light; when this occurs, I will make note of it in this section.

1 Nephi 1

VERSE 1

Being that Nephi starts by talking of his parents and uses the adjective "goodly," I want to make sure that I understand the meaning of the word because he also uses the word "therefore," which ties "goodly" to "taught somewhat in all the learning" of his father.

I select the word "goodly" and tap on Define, and a small window appears, providing two definitions. The current meaning of the word in the primary definition would not apply to the verse. However, the second archaic definition could possibly apply, especially the words "excellent" and "admirable."

I decide to see how the 1828 Webster Dictionary defines the word. There I find several definitions and decide to copy and paste them in a note that is connected to the word "goodly."

To further my research, I used Strong's Concordance and found that the word was used in the Old and New Testaments and was usually tied to physical appearance.

After my research and pondering the meaning in the context it is used, I added the following to the note: "goodly may also mean distinguished, esteemed, or respected—an allusion to both moral and spiritual status."

As I pondered why Nephi would start his record with mentioning his goodly parents, I began to wonder what educational systems existed in 600 BC. Using Google, I found wonderful information about how children were educated in Ancient Israel. I learned that they were taught in six subjects covering various aspects of their religion, but most children did not learn to read or write.

I noted and read the various links in footnote 1d in Related Content.

Related Content

School in Ancient Israel

In Ancient Israel, the child would be taught from the six broad subject areas into which the Mishna is divided, including:

- **Zeraim** ("Seeds"), dealing with agricultural laws and prayers
- **Moed** ("Festival"), pertaining to the laws of the Shabbat and the Festivals
- **Nashim** ("Women"), concerning marriage and divorce
- **Nezikin** ("Damages"), dealing with civil and criminal law
- **Kodashim** ("Holy things"), regarding sacrificial rites, the Temple, and the dietary laws
- **Tohorot** ("Purities"), pertaining to the laws of purity and impurity, including the impurity of the dead, the laws of ritual purity for the priests (Kohanim), the laws of "family purity" (the menstrual laws)

Related Content

including the impurity of the dead, the laws of ritual purity for the priests (Kohanim), the laws of "family purity" (the menstrual laws)

Despite this schooling system, **many children did not learn to read and write.** It has been estimated that at least 90 percent of the Jewish population of Roman Palestine in the first centuries CE could merely write their own name or not write and read at all. Hezser, Catherine "*Jewish Literacy in Roman Palestine*", 2001, Texts and Studies in Ancient Judaism; 81. Tuebingen: Mohr-Siebeck, at page 503.

The literacy rate was about 3 percent. Bar-Ilan, M. "*Illiteracy in the Land of Israel in the First Centuries C.E.*" in S. Fishbane, S. Schoenfeld and A. Goldschlaeger (eds.), "*Essays in the Social Scientific Study of Judaism and Jewish Society*", II, New York: Ktav, 1992, pp. 46–61

From my research and thinking about what I have learned, I concluded that Nephi's parents were people that were respected in the community not only because of their character but possibly because of their wealth. Because of their station in life, Nephi was schooled in the learning of his father, which was not the norm for most children. I could see how the Lord prepared Nephi to be a leader and to have the skills needed to record a sacred record.

I also highlighted the word "afflictions" and made a note stating, "Even the righteous suffer afflictions" and added the etymology of the word: "From the Latin *affligere*, infliction of pain or humiliation." I also added a tag called "Affliction."

VERSE 2

Nephi's reference to using the "language of his father" led me to want a better understanding of Reformed Egyptian. Eventually I found an excellent, lengthy explanation about the language and created a note connected to the entire verse and noted the reference.

I was also able to find examples of what the language looked like. I saved the examples in Evernote (see Tips and Tricks for information about Evernote). I created an Evernote link and then pasted that into the same note above.

VERSE 5

I made a note that Lehi was thinking of and serving others.

VERSE 6

Using Strong's Concordance and Joseph Smith—History, I studied what a "pillar of fire" was. I learned that it was the glory and presence of the

Lord and noted that Joseph Smith experienced the same thing. All of this was recorded in a note connected to this verse.

I also made a separate note connected to "as he prayed," stating, "Personal revelation came through prayer."

VERSE 12

I made a note stating, "Reading the scripture brings the Spirit of the Lord into my life."

VERSE 19

I tagged the verse with "Jesus Christ" and "Messiah."

VERSE 20

I tagged the verse with "Faith."

Jacob 5

Below is an excellent example of how much I use notes and outside resources. In addition, I use color highlighting to help keep clear what is being explained. I only mention a few verses to help illustrate what can be done.

VERSE 1

I underlined the verse and then made a note stating, "This chapter is the answer to verse 17 of the previous chapter." I also created a link to Jacob 4:17.

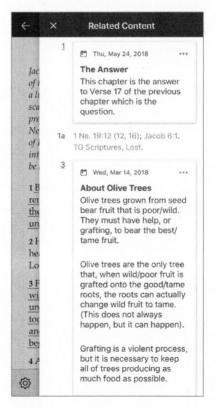

VERSE 3

I made a study about olive trees and from my research created a rather large note with details about how they are grown, the uniqueness of their roots, grafting, and why they are burned.

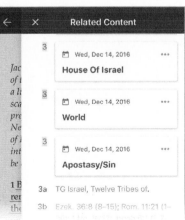

I also highlighted in different colors "olive tree," "vineyard," and "decay." Then I created a note for each, identifying what each one represented—House of Israel, World, Apostasy/Sin, respectively.

VERSE 4

I highlighted "master of the vineyard" and created a note identifying that term with Jesus Christ. I also highlighted "I will prune it, and dig about it, and nourish it" and created a note stating, "His work is to save the people."

I also highlighted "prune" and created a note stating, "To trim a tree or bush by cutting away the dead overgrown beaches of stems, especially to increase fruitfulness and growth."

VERSE 7

I highlighted "servant," "wild olive tree," and "cast them into the fire that they may be burned," highlighting each in a different color and creating a note for each—prophets, Gentiles, and Judgement/Exile/Death, respectively.

VERSE 22

I made a note regarding "poor spot of ground," titled "When one is put into a bad situation." In the note I stated, "The Lord knew it was the poorest spot of ground. Some people are given a difficult lot in life, but the Lord is aware of it."

I also added the following: "Even though it was the poorest spot of ground the Lord continued to nourish it. Though we may be in difficult circumstances the Lord is aware of it and continues to feed us. Despite the poor circumstances the fruit came about. Good things can come even though the situation itself may be bad because the Lord is aware of it and is there nurturing it."

Matthew 5

I have very long notes in this chapter, which were a result of studying the chapter over several months. Here I am going to touch on only a few.

VERSE 1

From the Gospelink, I found Hyrum Andrus's *Principles of Perfection and* copied and pasted a variety of his comments regarding this chapter.

VERSE 2

I created a note stating, "The sermon outlines the Law of the Gospel which instructs us on the steps to eventually becoming perfect even as Jesus Christ and our Heavenly Father are perfect.

I then created a summary of the entire chapter.

VERSE 3

I highlighted "poor in spirit" and created a long note. I remark that it means humility and occurs seven times in the KJV and fourteen times in the Book of Mormon. Then, using Strong's Concordance, I copied and pasted the meaning of the word in Greek and Hebrew into the note. This was followed by a long explanation regarding the phrase.

Poor in spirit
Humility

Occurs 7 times in the KJV and 14 times in the Book of Mormon

עָנָו
'ănâvâh, an-aw-vaw'; from; condescension, human and subjective (modesty), or divine and objective (clemency):—gentleness, humility, meekness

ταπεινοφροσύνη
tapeinophrosýnē, tap-i-nof-ros-oo'-nay; humiliation of mind, i.e. modesty:—humbleness of mind, humility (of mind, loneliness (of mind).

To be poor in spirit is to recognize that we are not self-sufficient spiritually (or materially, for that matter), but rather that we are always in debt to our Heavenly Father, from whom all blessings flow. In fact, our

To be poor in spirit is to recognize that we are not self-sufficient spiritually (or materially, for that matter), but rather that we are always in debt to our Heavenly Father, from whom all blessings flow. In fact, our posture before our God is as the needy, even as beggars. President Harold B. Lee spoke on this subject in the following way:

"To be poor in spirit is to feel yourselves as the spiritually needy, even dependent upon the Lord for your clothes, your food, the air you breathe, your health, your life; realizing that no day should pass without fervent prayer of thanksgiving, for guidance and forgiveness and strength sufficient for each day's need. If a youth realizes his spiritual need, when in dangerous places where his very life is at stake, he may be drawn close to the fountain of truth and be prompted by the Spirit of the Lord in his hour

a sad thing for one, because of his wealth or learning or worldly position, to think himself independent of this spiritual need. [Poor in spirit] is the opposite of pride or self-conceit. To the worldly rich it is that 'he must possess his wealth as if he possessed it not' and be willing to say without regret, if he were suddenly to meet financial disaster, as did Job, 'The Lord gave, and the Lord hath taken away; blessed be the name of the Lord.' (Job 1:21.) Thus, if in your humility you sense your spiritual need, you are made ready for adoption into the 'church of the Firstborn,' and to become 'the elect of God.'" (Stand Ye in Holy Places, pp. 343-44.)

1. Robert E. Wells
Mount and the Master

3a The Latin beatus is the basis of the English "beatitude," meaning "to be fortunate," "to be happy," or "to be blessed." TG Blessing.

VERSE 4

I highlight "mourn" and create a note stating, "Possibly to mourn for our sins. If we are humble we then will see ourselves in a different light and see the need to repent which leads us to mourn, to be sad and to ask forgiveness."

VERSE 5

I highlighted "meek" and created a note stating, "Submissive, gentle, quiet, obedient."

VERSE 13

Using *Verse by Verse: The Book of Mormon*, by Kelly Ogden and Andrew Skinner, I copied and pasted the authors' explanation about salt. I typed in the beginning of the note that salt is a token of the covenant.

SECTION FIVE

Putting the Power in Teaching

The steps involved in preparing a lesson or a talk are the same. Below I will go through the basic process of creating a lesson.

A lesson should be prepared a few weeks before the lesson is given.

PRAYER

Start and end with prayer each time you engage in preparation.

FINDING AND SAVING CONTENT

Suppose you are preparing a lesson on grace. There are many ways to begin the process of preparing the lesson, such as reading the manual; using the Topical Guide or Index, the Bible Dictionary, *Preach My Gospel*, or *True to the Faith*; and searching the Library. Wherever you decide to start, the process of saving the information in a notebook is the same.

Create a notebook with the name of the lesson by going to Library / Notes / Notebooks / plus sign.

I would suggest using the following format: title of lesson, class, date. Here is an example:

Grace – Gospel Doctrine, 1/20/19

Remember this is just an example. Perhaps a different order or format would better serve you.

You could leave the class and date off, but I have found it helps to have that information for further reference, and especially for talks. Unless the audience is different, giving the same talk in the same year to the same audience is probably not a good idea.

For talks, I put in the title and the name of the audience and date (e.g., Family History, Valley 3rd Ward 3/16/17). This is really helpful for missionaries and high councilors to help them remember in which wards they have given the talk.

If I were preparing this lesson, I would start with a thorough reading of the Sunday School manual. I would read each scripture mentioned in the manual. While reading the manual and the scriptures, I would be marking text; adding notes, tags, links; and using the Add to Notebook function as inspired. With each scripture I would be looking at the related content.

Since you are going to be adding more material to that notebook, make sure the list is sorted by most recent so your notebook will be at the top of the list.

As I continue to study, certain words or phrases may pop up in my mind. I would do a search on each of those in the Gospel Library.

I would also use the Citation Index to see the comments of various speakers regarding specific scriptures. If I find something, a note attached to the scripture would be created and added to the notebook.

In addition, I would use dictionaries and the Blue Letter Bible for further insight to the use of words. Also, do not forgot about the use of maps in the classroom.

EDITING

Ideally you have spent a few weeks praying, pondering, and searching for content and understanding.

You have also prayed for help and asked what is it that the class needs and how you can best meet the needs of the class.

When you are finished gathering all the information, say a prayer and then go to the notebook and begin reading through the material you have saved. Under the guidance of the Spirit, decide what to keep or discard and in what order to present the information, and add comments as inspired. To add a comment, tap on plus sign.

ARRANGING NOTES

Remember that notes in the notebook can be arranged. See explanation of how to arrange the order of the notes in Day 9.

DELETING A NOTE

Delete the content you have decided that you do not need.

When everything is in the order you want and comments and titles have been added, your lesson or talk is ready.

Use multi-screens and bookmarks to organize the order of what you want to share.

THIS IS THE LORD PREPARING YOU

At this point I want to stress that while you have prayed, researched, and organized your lesson in the notebook, it does not imply that you are now going to start at the top of the notebook when giving the lesson and cover all of the material.

All the above was preparing yourself; what you share with the class should be as directed by the Spirit. "And the Spirit shall be given unto you by the prayer of faith; and if ye receive not the Spirit ye shall not teach" (D&C 42:14). "Open your mouths and they shall be filled" (D&C 33:8).

USING YOUR ELECTRONIC DEVICES IN THE CLASSROOM

The devices that you hold in your hand are not only a powerful tool in studying the gospel and preparing lessons but also in presenting your material.

It is very helpful to a class when a map is projected on a screen. It is also helpful to project key scriptures from the lesson on a screen. I find it very helpful to be able to point to a word or phrase rather than just talk about it.

There is also an assumption that everyone in the classroom is literate. This is not always the case. There are people who suffer from reading disorders such as dyslexia, have visual problems, or perhaps have a limited vocabulary. Rarely will such a person admit to it. Projecting material on a screen can be very helpful not only to those that have such problems but also to those who do not.

I want to be careful here and not imply that you create a PowerPoint presentation and present it to class, advancing from slide to slide. Years ago I did that, and I have seen many others do the same. But that was before I repented and understood that it was the Spirit that directed the lesson and not Microsoft.

This does not mean you shouldn't prepare a few slides if so moved to do so. It does mean that once you are teaching the lesson the Spirit may direct to do otherwise.

Now, with the caveat out of the way, I am suggesting that you be prepared at all times to connect your device to a projector or large flat screen whenever it is possible.

This is not a difficult thing to do, but is beyond the scope of this book to teach how to become connected. However, if you need help, you can go to TheBusyLatterDaySaint.com, and there you will find videos and photos on how to do it.

It is important—no, *vital*—that you have your own cords and attachments. Preparing to project your device on a screen only to arrive at church and learn they cannot find the needed cord or that what you want is already being used by another person is not a great experience.

In addition, use the LDS Media app for visual material and project it on a screen. This is much better than using a visual from the building library because you can project it, making it much easier to see.

Also, do not depend on the internet. The internet at Church is slow, and the Church advises teachers to download their material so they do not have to depend on the internet (see https://www.lds.org/media-library/download-instructions).

When you are teaching and using your device in class to project on the screen as you move from scripture to scripture or general conference talks, you are showing others what you have learned in this book, and they will start using their devices to study the gospel.

There are times in class that a question will be raised and you and others in class may not have the answer. Project your device on the screen and do a search in the Gospel Library. You will be teaching how to use the search function to find answers.

You do not need to be walking around the class with a cord attached to your device the entire time. Simply have the cord attached to the screen and the screen on, and when needed, attach the other end of the cord to your device. It will take about ten seconds for your device to show up on the screen.

CONNECTING WITH CLASS MEMBERS

President Monson has reminded us, "The goal of gospel teaching . . . is not to 'pour information' into the minds of class members. . . . The aim is to inspire the individual to think about, feel about, and then do something about living gospel principles."[39]

By using text messages and social media, you can stay in contact with your class members. Encouraging them, providing something for them to think about during the week, share your testimony or personal experience tied into the upcoming lesson or to a recent past lesson.

MAKING YOUR MATERIAL AVAILABLE TO THE CLASS

Often I see people that have handouts for their class and wonder why they are not using a digital format rather than printing a handout. I think that it is a waste of paper and ink.

This does not mean you should not print a few copies, because there are people in the class who are not participating in the digital age. As you get to know your class, you will learn who does not use electronic devices or have a computer at home; give them a printed copy. For the others, do one of the following:

Project a QR code on the screen at the end of class so the class can scan it. When they scan it, they will be led to where you have the document stored on the internet. Then they can read the material on their device or print it out at home. Go to TheBusyLatterDaySaint.com to learn how to create a QR code.

Provide the class with a website that you have set up just for the class. These sites are easy to set up, free, and do not need to be fancy. On your site you will have a link to all your material. Most likely there is someone in your ward or branch that can help you set up a site and add links.

Have a private Facebook page just for the class, and list links to your material there. Again, someone in your unit can help you set that up.

Set up Slack (a private messaging service) for the class. Their basic service is free and has more than enough features to be useful to you. Not only is this a great place to store your material, but it is also a very easy

---

39. Thomas S. Monson, in Conference Report, Oct. 1970, p. 107.

way to communicate with class members during the week. You can find information about Slack at TheBusyLatterDaySaint.com.

The above are just a few ideas that can enable you to distribute and communicate with your class.

DOWNLOADING VIDEOS

If you are going to use a video from the Gospel Library in the classroom, it is best and advised to download it. This avoids any problems with bandwidth problems.

After finding a video you want to share, tap on the download icon, and the icon will be replaced with a clock showing how much time is left to complete the download. To view the video, go to Settings / Downloaded Media.

Also, you can use the LDS Media app, in which you can have available the same videos as in the Gospel Library along with the ability to trim them to the length you want.

This allows you to reduce a three-minute-long video down to just the one minute you want to show. See TheBusyLatterDaySaint.com for a video demonstration.

Missionary Work: Touching Lives in New Ways

These digital resources are a wonderful way to involve others in what you are learning and experiencing by sharing selected text with a member of the family, a neighbor, members of your Sunday School class, or on social media.

> "How beautiful are the feet of them that preach the gospel of peace, and bring glad tidings of good things!" (Romans 10:15)

> "And even so I have sent mine everlasting covenant into the world, to be a light to the world, and to be a standard for my people, and for the Gentiles to seek to it, and to be a messenger before my face to prepare the way before me." (D&C 45:9)

> "Sanctify the Lord God in your hearts: and be ready always to give an answer to every man that asketh you a reason of the hope that is in you." (1 Peter 3:15)

> "Every member is a missionary!"[40]

Members are encouraged to use the internet to flood the earth with testimonies of the Savior and His restored gospel. They should view blogs, social networks, and other internet technologies as tools that allow them to amplify their voice in promoting the message of peace, hope, and joy that accompany faith in Christ.[41] Certainly sharing the gospel has taken on new meaning in the digital age.

Elder David A. Bednar encouraged us to "sweep the earth with messages filled with righteousness and truth—messages that are authentic, edifying, and praiseworthy—and literally to sweep the earth as with a flood."[42] The Gospel Library has made it easy to share the gospel, to

---

40. David O. McKay, talk given to North British Mission, Mar. 1, 1961.
41. Handbook 2, 21.1.22 – "Internet."
42. David A. Bednar, "To Sweep the Earth as with a Flood," BYU Education Week address, Aug. 19, 2014.

have a tremendous impact upon the world that before today was thought impossible.

Elder Dieter F. Uchtdorf said, "With so many social media resources and a multitude of more or less useful gadgets at our disposal, sharing the good news of the gospel is easier and the effects more far-reaching than ever before. In fact, I am almost afraid that some listening have already sent text messages like 'He's been speaking for 10 minutes and still no aviation analogy!' My dear young friends, perhaps the Lord's encouragement to 'open (your) mouths' might today include 'use your hands' to blog and text message the gospel to all the world!"[43]

To follow the counsel of Elder Bednar and Elder Uchtdorf, you need to be using some social media sites. These include Facebook, Twitter, Pinterest, and Instagram, to name a few. It is not within the scope of this book to explain how to join the sites or download the apps. If you are not using social media and, after reading this chapter, want to start, then talk to a friend who is already using social media, and they can help you get started. I am going to assume you already are using social media.

When looking for help with these sites, I would suggest you find someone your own age to show you. If you do work with a young person, make sure they understand to go slow and allow you to tap and swipe instead of them showing you on their device so that you can learn.

SHARING

To share something that you are reading from the Gospel Library, select the text and, in the pop-up, tap on Share.

If you are sending a post to Facebook, select the text, tap on Share / Facebook. A pop-up will appear with your selection and the Church logo. Type a comment in the comment field and add a hashtag (see below). Before posting, you can also tap on the right arrow and decide who to share the post with. When you're done, tap on post.

For more detailed explanation on using the share function, see the Tips and Tricks chapter.

---

43. Dieter F. Uchtdorf, "Waiting on the Road to Damascus," *Ensign*. May 2012.

USING HASHTAGS

Hashtags are used in social media and now in some apps as a way of indexing comments or other material.

Hashtags are a powerful missionary tool when using social media. Hashtags in social media create a searchable link. If you click on a hashtag, you will be shown other posts that have used that same hashtag. This can become a powerful missionary tool.

For example, creating a post about the Church, a family event, the temple, or general conference with hashtags such as #LDS, #Temple, #BookofMormon or #GeneralConference provide a way for readers of your post to search for other related posts; this creates a research tool for non-members.

As mentioned above, Elder Bednar gave a powerful address a few years ago about social media. He said, "My beloved brothers and sisters, what has been accomplished thus far in this dispensation communicating gospel messages through social media channels is a good beginning—but only a small trickle. I now extend to you the invitation to help transform the trickle into a flood. Beginning at this place on this day, *I exhort you to sweep the earth with messages filled with righteousness and truth*—messages that are authentic, edifying, and praiseworthy—and literally to sweep the earth as with a flood."[44]

If you have not had the opportunity to read or hear his talk, I strongly suggest you do so. He provides excellent counsel on the use of social media and how it can be used for good along with examples and guidelines on its righteous use.

In his address, he encouraged members to use social media to spread the gospel and to use hashtags. He mentions the power of social media and the use of hashtags such as #BecauseofHim, #DidYouThinktoPray, and #LDSConf.

Hashtags do not need to be capitalized as shown above. The reason capitalization is used is to make it easier to read a long hashtag. There can be no spaces in a hashtag in social media.

When I use social media to send a gospel-related message, I use #JesusChrist, #Mormon, and #LDS. I do this so that a person searching about the Church will most likely search for the keywords "Mormon" and "LDS". I add #JesusChrist so when people read my messages they

---

44. Bednar, "To Sweep the Earth," emphasis added.

start making a connection subconsciously of Jesus Christ with the popular names of The Church of Jesus Christ of Latter-day Saints.

Note: With the August 16, 2018, announcement by the Church, "Name of the Church" (see https://www.mormonnewsroom.org/article /name-of-the-church), I have added #LatterDaySaint. I have decided to keep, at least for the time being, #Mormon and #LDS. The reason is that non-members of the Church will continue to search for either of those two hashtags.

Where do you find hashtags? People make them up. If, for example, you were posting a message about Easter, you could create a hashtag #EasterThoughts or #ThoughtsOnEaster. As your post is read by others and they share your post, the hashtags are also shared. If your post becomes popular, others will also start posting using the hashtag you created.

The Church has an excellent website page on social media (see https://www.lds.org/media-library/social). Within that information are links to hashtags the Church is using.

The General Authorities and auxiliary leaders all have hashtags connected to their name. You can search for them using the format below.

- First Presidency—#Pres followed by their last name.
- The Quorum of the Twelve and Seventies—#Elder followed by their last name.
- Presiding Bishopric—#Bishop followed by their last name.
- General Relief Society and Young Women presidencies—#Sister followed by their last name.
- General Young Men presidency—#Brother followed by their last name.

USING SOCIAL MEDIA OUTSIDE OF THE GOSPEL LIBRARY

While the Gospel Library is an excellent tool for sharing the gospel, you can also help spread the gospel outside of the Gospel Library, and it is easy and fun to do.

For example, as you leave the temple, take a picture of the temple and send the picture to your favorite social media site along with a short comment (e.g., "Had a great spiritual experience at the temple"). Add some hashtags—#Temple, #LDS, #JesusChrist, etc.—and post it. If you are in a hurry, leave off the photo (however, remember that posts with a photo get more attention) and just make your comment, add hashtags, and tap on Post.

Making a comment while watching general conference is not only an excellent way to share the gospel, but it also creates a journal of your thoughts about the conference, which can be automatically transferred to a journaling app, such as DayOne. See TheBusyLatterDaySaint.com for a video on how to transfer Twitter postings to your journal.

Share uplifting stories that you come across on the internet. Perhaps you find a touching story about someone that did a good deed. Posting the link to the story and adding a short comment with appropriate hashtags will inspire others to do good.

Do your comments have an impact? Yes, they do! Do they aid in spreading the gospel, in doing missionary work? Yes, they do! True, you most likely will never know the impact a message or post has on the world, but that should not matter. Simply by sharing you are "doing much good in this generation" (D&C 6:8) and helping to "sweep the earth as with a flood" (Moses 7:62).

I encourage you to be actively involved in social media following the guidelines given by Elder Bednar.

To get started, use Google to find information about getting started with social media or talk to a friend. Also, there are books on using social media in general, and specifically for the gospel there is *Sharing the Gospel through Social Media* by Erin Ann McBride, *101 Ways to Hasten the Work Online* by Larry Richman, and *The Virtual Missionary* by Greg Trimble. All are available through Deseret Book and other retailers.

MESSAGES AND MAIL

When we think of missionary work, the tendency is to think of finding someone that has not been introduced to the gospel. While that is very important, it is only part of it. There are those that are members and have strayed for various reasons, or those that are struggling and trying to hold on, who need missionary work as well. Ministering by the priesthood and Relief Society are also part of missionary work.

While the name of the home and visiting teaching program has changed to ministering, the following quote by Harold B. Lee still applies. He said, "Missionary work is but home teaching (ministering) to those who are not now members of the Church, and home teaching (ministering) is nothing more or less than missionary work to Church members."[45]

Missionary work can take place within the classes we teach. President Monson has reminded us "The goal of gospel teaching . . . is not to 'pour information' into the minds of class members. . . . The aim is to inspire the individual to think about, feel about, and then do something about living gospel principles."[46]

Sharing spiritual insights with others may appear to be a small thing, but the Lord has reminded us, "And out of small things proceedeth that which is great" (D&C 64:33).

If you teach a youth or adult Sunday School class, you can share a scripture that is tied in with the lesson or your favorite scriptures for the day. You could also share what the lesson is for next week. This is a great way to inform those who were absent the previous Sunday and to also remind the others. This also applies to Relief Society, priesthood, Young Women, and the Aaronic Priesthood. It is also a great way to stay in touch and teach the families you minister to.

To send a quote from the Gospel Library to a group message or email, select the text then tap on Share in the pop-up. Then tap on either Message, for a text message, or Mail, for an email. You will then be taken to the appropriate app. Regardless of the app, the selected text will be inserted along with the reference and a link. In the "To" field, type in the name of the group you created (for how to create a group in contacts, see below) and then tap on Send.

CREATING A GROUP

Before creating a group, make sure that all the contacts in your group have both an email address and mobile phone number so that you can send messages via texting or email.

iOS
- Log into www.icloud.com using your Apple ID and password.
- Select Contacts.
- Click the plus icon in the bottom left-hand corner.
- Select New Group.

---

45. Harold B. Lee, Improvement Era, Dec. 1964, p. 1078.
46. Thomas S. Monson, Conference Report, Oct. 1970.

- Name the group "Gospel Doctrine Class" or "Gospel Doctrine" or "GD" and save it.
- Go to All Contacts.
- Start dragging and dropping their names into the new group you created.
- When you are done, log off.

Open Contacts on your iPhone, then tap Groups in the upper left-hand corner of the screen, and the group your created will be listed on the next screen.

Note: There are also third-party apps in iOS that make the above process much easier. Two that I like for iOS are Simpler Pro and Interact. Go to the App Store and check them out.

Android

- Open the Contacts app.
- Find a contact you want to add to the group.
- Tap on Details.
- Tap on Edit at the top.
- Scroll down to Groups.
- Scroll down to the bottom.
- Tap on Create Group.
- Type the name of the group.
- Tap on Create.
- Tap on Save.

Once you have created a group with the first contact, find other contacts to add to the group.

- Go to the contact.
- Tap on Edit.
- Tap on Groups.
- Tap on the name of the group you previously created.
- Tap on the back arrow in the upper left-hand corner.
- Tap on Save.

GETTING NAMES FROM LDS TOOLS TO YOUR CONTACTS

Sending an email or text message to only one person from within LDS Tools is very simple. Find the name, and then do the following:

iOS
To send a text message

- Tap on the phone number.
- Tap on Send Text Message.
- Type your message, and send.

To send an email

- Tap on the email address.
- Type your message, and send.

Android
To send a text message

- Tap and hold the phone number.
- Tap on Send text message.

To send an email

- Tap on the email address.
- Tap on the email app you want to use.
- Type your message, and send.

If you want to send a message or email to more than one person, you can make a list in LDS Tools and send your message or email using that list.

However, there are a few reasons I would recommend not doing so. Not everyone puts their cell phone number in the church directory, or they still use a landline phone in addition to cell phones. Currently you can only enter one phone number in the LDS directory, and there is no way to designate if it is a cell phone or landline.

Another problem is if you are going to use text messaging and send to more than ten people, it won't work because messages have a limit of ten recipients. There are apps that help overcome the ten-person limit. I like to use Groups for iOS. For Android and iOS there is GroupMe. What the apps do is automatically divide the list into groups of ten and then send the message out; very slick.

Using email is a problem because not everyone has email (yes, hard to believe), they may not put their email address in the LDS Tools, or worse, while they may have email, there are people that only check their email once a week or even once a month.

In addition, you may want to use third-party apps that you can send contact information to, such as Slack, but you would not be able to do it from LDS Tools.

Lastly, I prefer to use my own third-party email app rather than the iOS or Android system email apps. At this point in time you do not have the choice in LDS Tools for iOS to choose which email app you want to use.

Here is how to share a contact in LDS Tools to your contact app.

iOS
- Open LDS Tools.
- Find the person you want to add to your contact list.
- There is an arrow to the right of person's name and phone number.
- Tap on Add to Contacts.
- Scroll down if needed to Create New Contact, and tap on it.
- Check if everything transferred over correctly, and add any additional information.
- Tap on Done when you are finished.

Note: I would suggest when adding members of your ward or branch to put the name of the unit in the company name field, making it easy to locate all unit members you have in your contacts.

Android
- Open LDS Tools.
- Find the person you want to add to your contact list.
- Tap on the name of the person at the bottom of the screen under Household Members.
- Tap on the option menu icon in the upper right-hand corner.
- Tap "Create a new contact."
- A window providing some information will appear.
- Tap on OK.

- Check if everything transferred over correctly, and add any additional information.
- Scroll down to Groups if you want to add the person a group.
- Tap on Save when done.

ON THE SUBJECT OF TEXTING AND EMAILING

When communicating with anyone, it is always best to use the mode they prefer. I ask someone how they prefer to be contacted, and then I use that mode.

Most people prefer text messages, but you may have someone that prefers email or Facebook Messenger, Snapchat, etc. There maybe even some that still prefer receiving a call on their phone.

LDS PAMPHLETS (IOS AND ANDROID)

A beautiful selection of pamphlets to show and share.
See TheBusyLatterDaySaint.com for instructions on how to share.

DOWNLOADING VIDEOS

As stated in the previous chapter, but worth repeating, if you are going to use a video from the Gospel Library in the classroom, it is best and advised to download it. This avoids any problems with bandwidth.

After finding a video you want to share, tap on the download icon, and the icon will be replaced with a clock showing how much time is left to complete the download.

To view the video, go to Settings. Then, for iOS, go to Downloads, and, for Android, go to Downloaded Media.

Becoming a Digital Master

There are many great apps available for iOS and Android.

It is way beyond the scope of this book to provide extensive details on how I use the apps in conjunction with my scripture study and in my daily life.

However, if you go to TheBusyLatterDaySaint.com, there are videos to show how I use them.

Below are the ones that I use daily in life to help keep me on track in studying the scriptures. As I mention below, there are other apps that serve the same purpose, but these are my favorites.

DATA STORAGE AND RETRIEVAL

EVERNOTE (iOS AND ANDROID)

Evernote is a very popular application with over 150 million users that runs on every platform and syncs with all devices (there are some limits depending on your plan). The application is used to store, organize, and retrieve information quickly.

The biggest advantage to using Evernote is the indexing and search feature. Every single word is indexed, even text in PDF and photos (available on the higher plans).

Finding a note is so easy because of the indexing. All you have to remember is just one word in the document and you will be able to find it.

They have a basic plan that is free, and for most people that will suffice. I subscribe to the premium plan because of the additional features it provides. Go to evernote.com and click on Explore to see their plans.

I use Evernote in conjunction with the Gospel Library. The reason to use Evernote with the Gospel Library is twofold.

First, you cannot add photos to notes in the Gospel Library. By using Evernote, I can create a link from a photo or diagram in Evernote to a note in the Gospel Library.

Second, there are times that I have a very long article that I want in a note in the Gospel Library, and by using Evernote I can make it happen.

A link is automatically created for every note in Evernote. The link can be copied and pasted in a note in the Gospel Library. I can then click on the link in the note in the Gospel Library and be transferred quickly to the document in Evernote, and when I am done, I can return quickly to the Gospel Library.

Many people also use Evernote for doing family history research, and a book has been written on how to specifically use Evernote for that purpose. You can find *How to Use Evernote for Genealogy* by Kerry Scott on Amazon.

Evernote for Android also offers the ability to handwrite notes, which is discussed later in this chapter.

Evernote has so much to offer, and it is beyond the scope of this book to cover everything it can do. I suggest you download it and start using it. Also there are many excellent books available on how to use Evernote.

The guru of how to use Evernote in general is Brent Kelly, and he wrote *Evernote Essentials,* an excellent book to help you to build a solid foundation of why and how to use Evernote.

Some people like to use OneNote by Microsoft instead of Evernote, which also runs on every platform. It does have its advantages, but I continually go back to Evernote. Google "OneNote vs. Evernote" to see how some people have compared the two apps.

HANDWRITING NOTES ON A DIGITAL DEVICE

You can use your mobile device to take handwritten notes. You can use your smart phone or tablet. Obviously, taking notes on a smartphone, while possible, is not as comfortable as using a tablet. There are smartphones that come with a stylus, such as the wonderful Samsung Galaxy Note 9. I use my iPad almost daily to take handwritten notes.

NOTABILITY (iOS)

There are many times that I want a pen and paper so I can write notes and draw out ideas on paper. With this application, I can take notes or draw out my ideas and then save them to Evernote, or the application can convert my handwriting to text, which I can then copy and paste in the Gospel Library.

It also has recording capability so one can record the lecture and take notes at the same time. What is cool is that later, when reviewing the notes, you can have the recording start exactly at a specific word in the note. This is a feature that is excellent for students. I personally do not use it.

Another excellent feature—which is why I switched from Good Notes (see below)—is their global search capabilities. The app indexes all printed text AND handwriting throughout all the notebooks. You can do either a global search or a search within a note.

GOOD NOTES (iOS)

Another good app is Good Notes, which has many of the same features as Notability, except for recording. What is really nice is you can drag your handwriting over to the note in the Gospel Library, and as you drag, the handwriting coverts to text.

There is a problem when converting from handwriting to text: your handwriting. You may have to write a little slower to write more clearly. With that said, I do not have great handwriting and the conversion is very good except for capitalization.

Some of my words end in all caps or a mixture of upper and lower case. If you find that you have a problem with that, there is an app for that. Text Case (iOS) is an excellent app with plenty of options. Also, Drafts (iOS) has an action that will also take care of the problem, although it does not have all the options Text Case has. Check out the App Store for other options.

For Android there is a large pick of apps that will take care of the capitalization problems. Drafts is not available for Android.

All the apps for either iOS or Android are easy to use. You can take your jumbled capitalization text and have it all in lower case in seconds. There is also a website that will convert the text; go to http://www.text-caseconverter.com.

LECTURENOTES (ANDROID)

I have not used this app, but from the feedback and reviews I have seen it is one of the top-selling handwriting apps for Android. This does not have handwriting indexing.

However, there is an easy work around. Export the note(s) to Evernote, and Evernote will index the handwriting.

I have not been able to find a handwriting app that indexes the handwriting for Androids. It may exist, but I have not found one.

JOURNALING

It is important that you have a place to keep a journal. What is even more important is to have a place to not only keep a journal but to be able to retrieve journal entries.

Evernote is used by many to keep a journal. I am sure that if you search Google for "using Evernote to keep a journal," you will find plenty of information. I prefer to use a dedicated journaling app. Below is what I recommend.

DAYONE (iOS AND ANDROID)

This I use every day. It is a very powerful and highly rated journaling application. The application syncs with all my devices and offers features such as the weather the day the entry was made, voice recording, and creating books, to name a few—you cannot get those when using a pen-and-paper journal or using Evernote or OneNote.

They have excellent support and answer your questions often in the same day—sometimes even in the same hour. Plus, they have frequent updates, and the app just keeps getting better and better.

For Apple lovers, they also offer an app for the iWatch, which is really helpful.

I have introduced many people to this application, and they always comment on how much they enjoy using it and how it has changed their approach to journaling. To learn more, go to http://help.dayoneapp.com/day-one-2-0/popular-feature-requests and click on *Premium Only* for the different plans.

• •

KEEPING TRACK OF TO-DOS

THINGS (iOS)

If your mind is a steel trap so that you never forget to do things, then you do not need a to-do application; as for me, I cannot live without one. Things helps me to remember the important things in my life. There are several great iOS applications in this genre, and I have used them all. This is my favorite. Go to https://culturedcode.com/things to learn more or search Google to find reviews of other apps.

In connection with the Gospel Library, I will sometimes share a verse or a title of an article or talk with Things and make a note in Things to read the attachment at a later date. Then I do not forget to follow up, and clicking on the link in Things will take me directly to the item in the Gospel Library.

There is also a built-in to-do app in iOS called Reminders and Reminder for Android. They do not have all the bell and whistles that Things and other third-party apps have, but they may be just what you need.

• •

MANAGING AN ORGANIZATION

TRELLO (iOS AND ANDROID)

The main concept of this application is to help manage projects.

I use the application to help share with branch leadership all that is taking place with investigators and members that are less active. Using Trello for missionary work saves me time personally and in branch council meetings.

I also used it to manage dinners for the missionaries. Many people also use it for managing their family histories.

If I were a bishop or held another Church leadership position, I would be using Trello and ask all of my leaders to do the same. It saves a lot of time in meetings. There is also another app that is excellent for this purpose and is used by some wards. The app is called Asana (iOS and Android).

For more information about Trello, go to https://trello.com, and for Asana, go to http://asana.com.

PDF EXPERT (iOS)

With this application, I can create, store, and modify PDF files, and everything syncs among my mobile devices and Mac. I store patriarchal blessings, manuals, and various Church documents, such as the doctrinal exposition on the Father and the Son by the First Presidency and the Twelve, June 30, 1916. Evernote and PDF Expert each have particular features that are not common between the two. There are times that PDF

Expert better fits what I am trying to do. I could write a whole chapter on each of the apps, but it is beyond the scope of this book.

For Android, you might want to check out Squid, which allows you to take notes and mark up PDF documents.

SCANNER PRO (iOS)

This app allows me to scan documents directly into my phone. Mobile scanning applications do not scan as we understand scanning (i.e., placing a document on a glass plate or running it through a scanner). Instead the application uses the camera to take a picture of the document. So why use mobile scanner software? Because the application will take a better picture of the document, will automatically align the document for the best picture, and allow you to edit or modify the document to gray scale, black and white, or color, and save the picture as a PDF document all while saving you time.

This app will also automatically send the document to Evernote.

The application produces a better document when scanning a book. As you have experienced when taking a photo of a page in a book, the text near the binding is bent and sometimes hard to read. This application solves that problem.

If you are involved in doing family history research, having the ability to scan important family documents or scanning pages from a valued family book is of great value.

If you use Evernote, they also have a scanner called Scannable (iOS), and you may want to try that out also.

For Android, there is CamScanner and Adobe Scan. Adobe Scan is also available for iOS.

LDS-SPECIFIC APPS

PRODUCED BY THE CHURCH (iOS AND ANDROID)

DOCTRINAL MASTERY

This is a Church application that helps you to memorize the one hundred seminary scripture mastery passages. You can also add scriptures that are not part of those one hundred. The app can be found in your Gospel Library in Settings / Featured Apps. Tap on the app you want, and it will take you to the store so you can download it.

LDS MEDIA LIBRARY

This application contains Church images, music, and videos. The main features are the ability to create a playlist and to trim videos. These are great for preparing a lesson. The app can be found in your Gospel Library in Settings / Featured Apps. Tap on the app you want, and it will take you to the store so you can download it.

With this app you do not need to visit the building library to get visual material.

BOOK OF MORMON

There is a separate Book of Mormon app. I suggest you download it. If you want to share the Book of Mormon with someone, do a hard press and then tap on Share and pick the method you want to use to share it. Remember to make a comment, such as your testimony, before sending it.

When you open the app, there is a comment icon in the lower left-hand corner. Make sure you point that out to the person you are sharing the app with. When they tap on it, there are three items to help the reader to learn more:

- Learn more online.
- Ask a question.
- Worship with us.

The Android does have the app available, but there is no way to share it. However, the app does have the Learn More option. Tap on the option menu / Learn More.

BIBLE VIDEOS

While all the videos in this app are in the Gospel Library, the app does provide an interactive map, which may help when teaching young children.

LDS MUSIC

This contains the official hymns of the Church, the Children's Songbook, Additional Songs for Children, and Youth Theme Music. It contains most of the sheet music; some songs only have the words because of copyrights.

You also have audio. With audio you can pick Music, Vocals, or Music Only.

I cannot tell you how many times I have used this when in a meeting that starts with an opening song and I am able to provide accompaniment. Also, there have been times that I have been asked to play piano and there were no hymn books available in the room, so I used my iPad.

You can even make a playlist.

LDS TOOLS

I assume that you are already using this. If not, download it now. It provides a directory of the stake and each ward in your stake. Temple schedules, missionary information, and a missionary referral system, plus much, much more.

LDS YOUTH

If you work with the youth or have children at home, this app is a must. It puts at your fingertips the latest youth content by the Church. Download it and see all that it has to offer.

MORMON CHANNEL

The Mormon Channel is the media channel of The Church of Jesus Christ of Latter-day Saints. It contains videos, music, talks, quotes, and a whole lot more.

THE TABERNACLE CHOIR

This is great for a Sunday afternoon or any other time. It has music streaming, videos, Music and the Spoken Word, and a Sacred Music Library, plus more.

FAMILYSEARCH MEMORIES

This app is great for family gatherings. Take pictures directly from your grandmother's photo album and then record her as she tells about the photos. When you are done, you can upload all of it to FamilySearch and attach to the appropriate person.

FAMILYSEARCH TREE

You do not need to be at home in front of a computer or go to the Church Family History Library to work on family history. You can do it at any place or time that you have Wi-Fi access to the internet. There is no excuse for not being able to work on family history. The same principle that applies to studying the scriptures is true with family history: line upon line, precept upon precept, here a little and there a little (D&C 128:21). Over time, it adds up.

LDS PAMPHLETS

This app provides interactive versions of the pamphlets published by the Church. There are ways that can you can also share them with others. See TheBusyLatterDaySaint.com for more information.

• •

THIRD-PARTY APPS

DAILY VERSE

I love this app. My wife and I use this application every morning while having breakfast. Each day it provides a quote from a scripture, then to expand on the theme of the scripture, a comment from a General Authority, a hymn, and a video. Go to the Apple or Play Store and search for LDS Daily Verse.

LDS 67 LANGUAGE SCRIPTURES

Study the scriptures in two languages at the same time. You have a choice of sixty-seven languages. Pick two and see them side by side.

• •

THE MOST IMPORTANT TOOL

PRAYER & THE HOLY GHOST

I saved this for last because it is the most important of all the other tools, and it is free, available to every individual and extremely powerful. Starting scripture study with prayer is not only vital; it is also necessary. We have been commanded to pray for help and guidance: "Ask, and it shall be given you; seek, and ye shall find; knock, and it shall be opened unto you" (Luke 11:9).

The Lord has blessed us with technological tools to hasten his work. The words of President Spencer W. Kimball ring true: "I believe that the

Lord is anxious to put into our hands inventions of which we laymen have hardly had a glimpse."

However, using the tools alone will bring limited success. Effective study always begins with prayer (*Preach My Gospel*, 17), and listening to the Holy Ghost is absolutely vital.

Using the technology tools that Lord has provided combined with the power of prayer and the Holy Ghost, our ability to comprehend and apply the scriptures to bless our lives and the lives of others is increased in ways never before thought possible.

Tips and Tricks

TABLETS

If you have an iPad Pro, then use split screens. For example, I open the Gospel Library and Notability so that as I study the scriptures and as I receive impressions I am ready to write them in Notability without having to switch applications, and if I so desire, I can have my handwritten notes converted to text and drop them into a note in the Gospel Library.

There are many styluses you can use, but I prefer using the Apple Pencil. The pencil only works with an iPad Pro and the 9.7-inch iPad that was introduced in March 2018.

There are various Android tablets that also have split screens capability, and there are many excellent styluses for those tablets also. I have an Android phone but not a tablet. However, I have had the opportunity to use one from time to time, and they have some really great features.

MAKING A CONNECTION

If you have a tablet that only uses Wi-Fi and you are out and about and want to use your tablet, there are several things you can do. Stop at any Starbucks or fast-food restaurant and use their Wi-Fi. No, you do not need to purchase anything. Just remember that this is not a private Wi-Fi, so do not do any financial transactions or any other thing you want to keep private. I feel that using it with the Gospel Library is fine. Others may disagree.

Or you can create a hotspot. This will connect the tablet to your phone and use the cellular connection on your phone.

iOS
- Go to Apple Settings / Personal Hotspot, and turn Personal Hotspot on.
- Go to your iPad or Android tablet, and go to Wi-Fi.
- Find the name of your phone, and tap on it.

Android
- Swipe down on your home screen.
- Tap on the settings icon / Connections / Mobile Hotspot and Tethering / Mobile Hotspot.

- Go to your iPad or Android tablet and go to Wi-Fi. There you will see the name of your phone. Tap on it.

DICTATION FUNCTION

iOS and Android devices have a microphone to the left of the space bar (on the newer iPhones, such as the Xs, the icon is in the bottom right-hand corner). I suggest you use the built-in microphone instead of typing when you are in an application such as email or text messages or are using notes in the Gospel Library. Tap on Mic, and start speaking. Keep in mind that this would not work well in a noisy room or where you want some privacy.

This does take a little practice because you cannot just talk because it will come out as one long sentence. You must mention commas, periods, etc. Below is an example.

This is the sentence I read:

Thank you for your response. Please see the attached PMP document. I have discussed the proposal with my partners (John Smith & Bill Franks) and they were very positive in their remarks.

Look forward to meeting you on February 15, 2018 at 2 pm.

Now here is what I had to say. The brackets indicate additional instructions.

Thank you for your response. [period] Please see the attached [all caps] PMP document. [period] I have discussed the proposal with my partners [open parenthesis] John Smith [ampersand] & Bill Franks [closed parenthesis] and they were very positive in their remarks. [new line] [new line]

Look forward to meeting you on February 15, 2018 at 2 pm. [period]

The application does know to capitalize the beginning of a sentence and knows common proper nouns and will capitalize as needed. It is also familiar with dates.

And this was the result.

Thank you for your response. Please see the attached PMP document. I have discuss the proposal with my partners (John Smith & Bill France) and they were very positive in the remarks.

Look forward to meeting you on February 15, 2018 at 2 PM

Yes, there were some errors, but they are easy enough to correct.

Speaking is much faster than typing even with correcting the errors. The average person types at 40 words per minute using a standard keyboard for a desktop computer (possibly musch slower when using their thumbs on their smartphone), while the average person speaks between 125 and 150 words per minute.

As mentioned earlier, it takes practice, but it will be worth it because of the time it saves. In a short time you will be become a pro. I suggest you search Google for more information on how to use Siri and OK, Google.

REMINDERS

As mentioned in the previous chapter, having an app that can help you remember things is important. Here are instructions on how to add a reminder to the built-in apps.

You're going to send a scripture to a reminder, to help remind you to memorize it.

iOS
- Mark the scripture.
- Tap on Share / Reminders.
- Place the cursor at the beginning of the content.
- Add comments about what you want to remember to do with the scripture.
- Change the options if desired.
- Tap on Add.

Note: In Options, reminders can be set up to repeat at various intervals, and alarms can be set. You can also set a reminder to remind you when you arrive at a certain location.

Android
- Mark the scripture.
- Tap on Share / Keep (make sure to download Google Keep first).
- Provide a title if you so desire.
- Tap on Close App if a warning appears.
- In the title field, type what it is you want to remember to do with the scripture.
- Tap on Save.
- Return to the Gospel Library using the system's back arrow.

NOTES

Both iOS and Android have built-in note applications.

During a lesson, listening to a talk, or at any other time, make notes. Then peruse the notes and decide what you want to do with them. Perhaps it is a reminder of something that you should be doing in your daily life, something concerning your family, or something that requires some repentance.

Then decide where you want to copy and paste the note (in a to-do application, the Gospel Library Notebook, etc.).

For iOS users, I strongly recommend using Drafts, which is a great app to capture notes of all kinds, and then you can send the notes to various other apps. If I have a long text message to send, I always create it in Drafts first so I can easily see the entire note and make corrections, and then with a tap it sends it to my message app. Also, perhaps you know of the frustration of starting to create a text message and then in the middle of the message you get a phone call or interpreted by someone, and when you go back to your message you find what you typed is gone and have to start over. That will never happen if you're using Drafts.

As mentioned in the previous chapter, if you have a tablet there are many excellent note-taking apps available.

In addition, there are several Android phones that come with a stylus, for example, the Samsung Galaxy Note 9, which enables you to handwrite notes. Currently iPhones do not have handwritten note capability.

USING LINKS

Pasting links from websites in notes and notebooks is very useful.

iOS
- Simply tap on a link and be taken to a source outside of the Gospel Library, and then another tap in the upper left-hand corner takes you back to the Gospel Library.

Android
- Touch and hold your finger on the link, and the entire link will be highlighted and a window will pop up. Tap on Browser. If you are offered other choices (for example, Evernote or Chrome), pick the one you want, and you will be taken to the document. To return to the Gospel Library, use the Android system's back arrow.

LINKING

When you think of linking, you most likely think of a link to a website. There are also ways to link one app with another.

For example, I can send email to my to-do app, Things 3. I open the email, tap on the menu, and then tap on Send to Things 3. Next time I open Things 3, the link to the email will be in the body of the to-do.

When you send some content in the Gospel Library via a text message, a link is created to the content and placed in the message. When the recipient receives the message, they click on the link and are taken to the content in the Gospel Library, or if they do not have the Gospel Library installed, they are taken to the reference at lds.org.

Many applications now make it possible to create a link to a specific piece of content. For example, suppose in Evernote I have an article I read on the web about how dogs are better pets than cats. Now I want to share the note with my cat-lover friend. I tap on the note and get a link specifically to that note and then send my friend the link in a text message with my personal message, "See, this finally settles it."

When my friend receives the message, she taps on the link and there is my Evernote note for her to read and fume over.

The question you may have at this point is what does this have to do with the Gospel Library? Here is just one example.

Suppose you have an article in Evernote you saved from a website last year. While studying in the Gospel Library, you remember something about the article and think it might apply to the scripture you just read.

So you do a search in Evernote (very easy to do) and see that its related. You copy the link from the article into a note in the Gospel Library. The next time you read that scripture there will be a link in the note attached to that scripture. Tap on the note, and then tap on the link and read the article.

USING SIRI (iOS)

For the following to work, you need to make sure your have Siri activated. Go to the iPhone settings / Siri & Search. Make sure the following are set to on.

- "Listen for 'Hey Siri'"
- "Press Side Button for Siri"
- "Allow Siri When Locked"

Now that you have Siri activated, while listening to audio, you hear something that you want to study at a later time. Hold down the home button until Siri is activated; the audio will stop to allow you to talk to Siri. Then tell Siri to remind you about what you would like to study further.

For example, I am listening to Alma 9, and while listening something catches my attention. I hold the home button, and when Siri starts I say, "Remind me to take a look at Alma 9 verse 11 about His matchless power." Siri will convert your speech into text and place it in your reminder app.

A word of caution here: Siri is not a member of the Church, and like most non-members, she is not familiar with our vocabulary. Therefore, she most likely will not be correct in spelling words like Alma, Moroni, etc. When I said the above quote, it came out as follows: "Take a look at Almond nine verse eleven about his matchless power." Nevertheless, what it shows is enough to remind what I want to study further.

Siri is an excellent feature, though it has its negatives, and with some study, it can be valuable in helping to save time and be more efficient. Google "Siri" to learn more, or when you open Siri there is a small "?" in the lower left-hand corner; tap on it for suggestions, or you can simply say to Siri, "Show me what you can do" or ask "How can I use you?"

In the iPhone settings (not the Gospel Library Settings), you can pick various voices for Siri. Go to settings / Siri & Search / Siri Voice. Currently you can pick either a male or female voice with an American, Australian, or British accent.

With iOS 12, which was released in September 2018, Siri has not only greatly improved, but also a whole new world is opening up using Siri with the new Shortcut app. Anything on how to use it with the Gospel Library will be posted on TheBusyLatterDaySaint.com.

USING "OK, GOOGLE" (ANDROID)

First you need to setup "OK, Google." To know how to set up "OK, Google" on your phone, search Google for instructions. There are many different phones that use Android, and it is beyond the scope of the book to cover all of the Android phones.

Once you have "OK, Google" activated, if while listening to audio you hear something that you want to study at a later time, stop the audio and then say, "OK, Google," and say what you want to be reminded about.

For example, something catches my attention while I am listening to Alma 9. I stop the audio and say, "OK, Google. Remind me to take a look at Alma 9 verse 11 about His matchless power." A reminder will be set up to remind me about that note in the future.

Also, Google may be a member of the Church because Google spelled Alma and Moroni correctly when I tested it.

AUDIO

This is a wonderful feature. It helps you to make better use of your time, allowing you to listen while getting ready in the morning, exercising, working around the house, or while in the car. Do you struggle to find time to read the *Ensign*? No problem: listen while doing your morning walk. Because the Gospel Library uses professional narrators, it is really a very pleasurable listening experience.

You can pick a male or female voice and playback speed. You can also move back or forward ten seconds or scrub to find the exact place. If you only have time to listen to part of the content, you can pause it and continue listening at a later time. There is an option for continuous play, which will automatically continue to the next article or book. You can download the audio, which is a good idea if you are going to use it for a lesson so you do not have to worry if Wi-Fi is available.

To listen, pick a chapter from a scripture, manual, or magazine and tap on the audio icon at the bottom of the screen.

If while you are listening to the audio and your phone rings, the audio will stop to allow you to respond to the call. When you are finished, the audio will start from where it paused. If for some reason it does not resume, tap on the play icon.

iOS

If you do not see the audio icon, there are two ways to have it appear.

1. Tap anywhere on the screen and the icon will appear. This will only happen if you turned on Allow Fullscreen in the settings.
2. Scroll up the screen.

Tap on the audio icon, and at the bottom of the screen will be the audio player. Across the top of the player are the following icons: download, go back ten seconds, play, go forward ten seconds, and settings. Below these icons is the timeline. On the left is how much time has expired, and on the right how time is left. On the line is a colored vertical line that allows you to move (scrub) to a particular point in the audio. This is good if you are in a classroom setting and want to start the audio at a specific point.

Tap on the audio setting at the far right of the player to see your options. The first line shows the playback options. You can play the audio at 25 percent slower (.75x), normal speed (1x), 25 percent faster (1.25x), 50 percent faster (1.5x), and double (2x). I suggest that you try all of them.

The second line is to turn on or off Continuous Play, and the third line is to choose a male or female voice. When you are finished making changes, tap on Close in the upper left-hand corner. To play, tap on the play icon.

To download, tap on the download icon. Once it has finished downloading (takes only seconds), go to the title bar / Settings / Downloaded Media, and you will find the downloaded audio there.

Android

If you do not see the audio icon, scroll to the top of the content. You can also tap on the option menu in the upper right-hand corner and then tap on Play Audio. At the bottom of your screen is the audio player.

Across the top of the player is an *X* to close the player and an option menu. Tap on the option menu, and you'll see Audio Settings and Download.

Below the above icons you have icons for previous chapter, rewind ten seconds, play, forward ten seconds, and next chapter.

Tap on the options menu and then Settings. You will see four options. Tap on Playback Speed. Choose the playback speed you want. You can play at half the speed (.5x), normal speed (1x), 25 percent faster (1.25x) 50 percent faster (1.5x), or twice the normal speed (2x). I suggest playing with the options to see if there is something that you like.

The Continuous Play option will advance to the next article or chapter when the present article or chapter has ended. Tap on Main Voice to choose between a male voice, female voice, or Text-to-Speech. Text-to-Speech is a computer-generated speech rather than professional readers.

Tap on the options menu and then Download. Then confirm the download by tapping on Download again. Once it has finished downloading (takes only seconds), go to the main screen option menu / Settings / Downloaded Media, and you will find the downloaded audio there.

SECTION SIX

Conventions and Terminology

The following conventions and terminology are used throughout the book.

- The convention for the order of steps to take is the step separated by /. For example, Library / Notes / Tags means to start at the Library, then tap on Notes, followed by tapping on Tags.

- **iOS** is the operating system for Apple mobile devices.

- **Android** is the operating system developed by Google. If you do not have an Apple product, you likely have an Android. Some of the devices that use Android are Samsung and LG devices.

- **Option menu**: the three vertical or horizontal dots found on various screens.

- **Hamburger icon**: three horizontal lines found on various screens. Placing a finger on the icon drags an item in a list to a different position.

- **Ghosted** means a word or letter is faded rather than black or some other color, and it means the option is inactive. To become active, something needs to occur, such as selecting some text.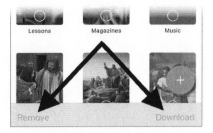

- **Collections** are the folders found in the Gospel Library main screen. For example, the Scriptures collection contains the scriptures along with the Topical Guide, Index, Maps, and other resources related to the scriptures.

- **Settings** allows you to customize the Gospel Library and set up syncing (back up).

iOS

Tap on the gear icon found in the lower left-hand corner.

Android

Found in the option menu in the upper right-hand corner.

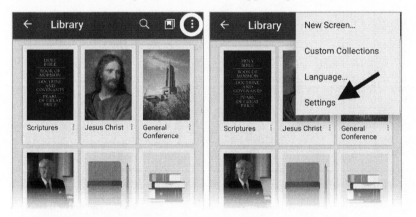

- **Tap the screen** means to touch the screen and then lift the finger in one movement.

- **Touch and hold** means to place your finger on the screen and not remove it until something appears on the screen such as a pop-up menu or the content appears to lift from the screen.

- **Title bar** is the colored bar across the top of screen. Depending on your device and settings, the title bar may vary in color and may be hidden. If it is hidden, double tapping on the screen will bring the title bar back.

- **Popup menu** is a small menu or content window that appears over the main screen after selecting some text. The popup then offers selection of other options. This is different from what is referred to as "windows" in a computer, which one can move about the screen.

- **Selected text** refers to a word that you have touched and held your finger on until a pop-up menu appears and the word is highlighted in light blue. If there is more than one word you want to select, then move the adjustment pins to select the entire text. The light blue highlighting is not permanent; its purpose is only to distinguish your selection from the rest of the text. If you tap anywhere on the screen, the blue highlighting will disappear.

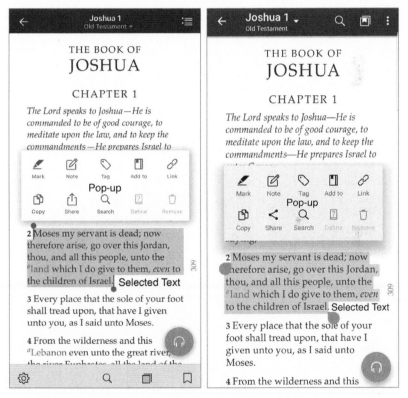

- **Marked text** is text that you have selected and marked with various styles and colors. This serves the same function as highlighting and underling printed text.

- **Drag** means to place your finger on the screen and move your finger in the direction given or to place your finger on an object and move in the desired direction.

- **Related content** contains all your notes, tags, links, and footnotes.

iOS

Tap on the icon is the upper right-hand corner.

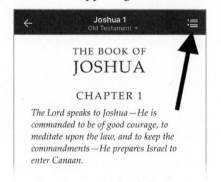

Android

Tap on the option menu in the upper right-hand corner; then tap on Related Content.

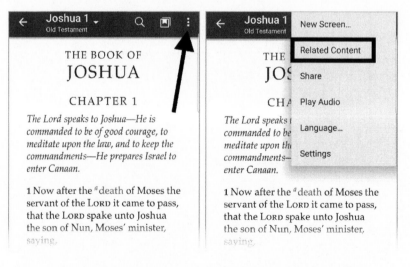

- **Clear field** or **clear item** is an *X* in a small circle or an *X* without the circle. Its use is very common in many applications today. Tap on the icon, and all the adjacent text will be deleted in one step. This is a better alternative then selecting the text and tapping the delete key on the keyboard, or even worse, tapping the delete key continually to delete each letter, which I often see people doing. It will, at times, also be next to an item such as a tag. Tap on *X*, and the tag is gone.

UI Awareness

INTRODUCTION

If you are new or fairly new to the using a mobile device, this chapter will be of great value to you.

If you feel comfortable moving about your mobile device, this chapter can still be of value because it will provide you with some insight on how to help others you know who struggle using mobile devices.

I have successfully used this method to help many learn the basics of using a mobile device.

Take your time with this chapter, especially if this new to you. Stop when you feel overwhelmed or tired, and continue at another time.

Once you have learned this technique, you will be able to manage very well on your own in using your mobile device.

It is important that you master this skill, and it is not hard to learn. You just need to continually remind yourself to use the technique instead of saying, "Help. I do not know what to do."

This skill is principle-based and is vital to interact with your mobile device as technology changes.

So stick with it, and soon you will do it automatically without giving it any thought; it will be second nature to you.

Watch two-year-olds using a mobile device, and you will find they use the same technique I am showing you today.

The brains of the youth today are not hardwired to use technology. The only difference between the older generation and the newest generation is they are not afraid to work at it, to experiment, and to learn from their experiences.

There are three principles:

PRINCIPLE ONE

Observe: scan the perimeter of the screen in a clockwise direction and notice the options available (meaning the icons and words).

PRINCIPLE TWO

Interact: tap on the most logical option, and see what happens.

PRINCIPLE THREE

Assess: Did you accomplish what you wanted to do? If not, start with Principle One and repeat the cycle.

So remember—observe, interact, and assess.

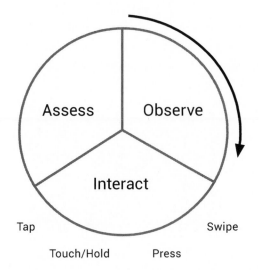

Principle Two requires some additional explanation. So I am going to explain Principle Two and then put all of the principles together as I work to solve a problem.

PRINCIPLE TWO_SCREEN INTERACTION

When you interact with the screen on your smartphone, you have four choices. Remember this could and most likely will change in the future as technology changes, which is why you are learning these skills.

Currently, not all these interactions are available on all devices.

The four choices are

- Tap
- Touch and hold
- Touch and press
- Swipe left, right, up, and down

For example, while in the Library I can do the following:

TAP

I tap on a collection, and I see what is in the collection.

TOUCH AND HOLD

I can touch and hold my finger on a collection. Some options occur at the bottom of the screen—Download All and Remove All. I have now learned that I can download or remove a whole collection. When doing the same thing for other collections, the results might be different.

For the Android, there is an option menu (the three vertical dots) on each collection. Tap on the option menu, and the same options as were available for the iOS are now available.

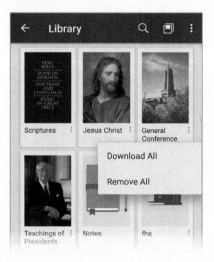

TOUCH AND PRESS

I touch and press one of the collections, and the same thing happens as touch and hold for iOS. Touch and press is not a valid option for Androids within the Gospel Library.

iOS

The ability to touch and press is called 3D touch on the iPhone. At this moment it is not available within the Gospel Library. However, it is used by other iPhone apps. By pressing down on an app icon, for example, a menu pops up, allowing for quicker access to the app's features.

Give it a try. Touch and press on the camera icon on your iPhone, and see what pops up. On my phone, I get the following:

Android

The Android's equivalent is called "quick app shortcuts." This feature is not available on all Androids.

Give it a try, and see if yours will respond. Do a touch and press on your phone icon.

You're probably wondering why I even mention 3D touch if it is not an available feature in the Gospel Library. The answer is simple. In the future it may be available, and you need to learn to do it. Also, while it is not available within the app, it is available on the library icon for the iPhone. Try it and see what happens.

With Android the quick app shortcuts are available on all the app icons. Get in the habit of trying this feature, and you will be surprised what will come up from time to time. I and others have often been delightfully surprised when we try 3D touch somewhere it is not expected and find some exciting things pop up.

SWIPE

If I am at the top of the Library, I can swipe down and then swipe up to see the full list of collections. There is no response when I swipe left or right.

• •

PUTTING THE PRINCIPLES TOGETHER

To interact with a device, there is a user interface (UI). The UI for mobile devices includes the icons, text, screen, and buttons. Observing all the options, interacting with the screen and assessing, is called UI awareness. This simple skill is what the geeks use, though most often they are unaware they are doing it.

The ability to observe, interact, and assess takes just a few seconds and will usually help you find what you are looking for.

Sometimes a function is deeply buried in an illogical location, but in general the choices are in plain sight and the icons are usually self-explanatory.

Being UI aware means that as technology changes—and it will—you will have no problem changing with it.

TAKING A TOUR OF THE LIBRARY

To understand what it means to be UI aware, I am going to use a screenshot from the Gospel Library and go through my thinking process.

All the screenshots are of an iPhone because it has more icons on the screen than the Android.

CREATING A CUSTOM COLLECTION

For this exercise, suppose that I, a new user to the Gospel Library, am wondering if it is possible to create a custom collection.

Our eyes tend to start in the upper left-hand corner when reading. This is why magazines place their most provocative or attention-grabbing content in that corner.

I begin in the upper left-hand corner and start observing what is available as I move clockwise around the perimeter of the screen and into the center.

In the upper left-hand corner of the top bar is an arrow pointing to the left. Reason and experience tell me that it most likely is a back arrow. I decide not to tap it.

In the middle of the top bar is the word Library. I tap, and nothing happens.

In upper right-hand corner is the word Edit. I tap it, and I notice things have changed. Starting in the upper left-hand corner again, I see the back arrow and, in the upper right-hand corner, I see Done.

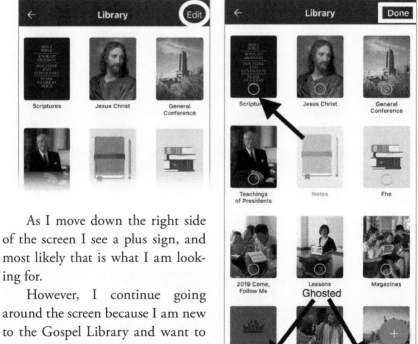

As I move down the right side of the screen I see a plus sign, and most likely that is what I am looking for.

However, I continue going around the screen because I am new to the Gospel Library and want to see what other options are available. I notice that Download and Remove are ghosted.

I now look at the middle of the screen and notice the collections have an empty circle on them, so I tap on one of the empty circles to see what happens.

Starting in the upper left-hand corner, I again go around the screen and notice at the bottom of the screen Remove and Download are no longer ghosted. It appears that I can remove or download collections.

I tap on the collection that I had previously tapped on and notice the check mark in the circle is removed.

From everything that I've seen, I can guess that the plus sign is the key to adding a collection.

Now I tap on the plus sign.

I am now being asked to type a collection name. I type "Gospel Doctrine Class."

Cancel	Create Collection	Save
Collection Name		
Add items to the collection for easy access.		

Cancel	Create Collection	Save
Gospel Doctrine Class		⊗
Add items to the collection for easy access.		

I again start in the upper left-hand corner and go around the screen and into the middle.

I notice the word Save in the upper right-hand corner and Done on the keyboard. It looks to me that either will complete the task. I decide to tap on Done, and now I am back to the Library and can see my new collection.

Note: In Androids, the collection can also be found in the option menu.

ADDING MATERIAL TO THE NEW COLLECTION

I have created a custom collection, but how do I add material to the collection?

Again, I start in the upper left-hand corner and go around the screen.

In the lower right-hand corner are three icons: a ribbon, two overlapping squares, and a magnifying glass.

BOOKMARKS

From my past experience, I am guessing that the ribbon icon is for bookmarks. To make sure, I tap on the icon, and a list of bookmarks appears. I again, starting in the upper left-hand corner, go around the screen and see Cancel, Edit, and History. It is clear what Cancel will do, so I tap on Edit and see what happens.

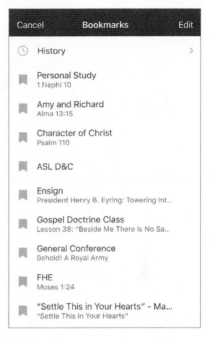

I tap on one of the red circles, and it appears that I can delete things from the list. I tap anywhere on the screen, and the delete option is removed. I see hamburger icons on the right of each item. I tap one, and nothing happens. I touch and hold, and the item appears to pop up. While keeping my finger on the screen, I slide up or down and see that I can arrange the items. I tap on the name of one of the bookmarks and learn that I can rename the bookmark. I tap on the back arrow and then on Done.

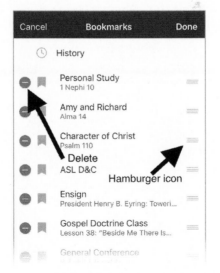

HISTORY

Now I tap on History, and a list of where I have been on a given day appears. Now I have learned where to find my history. I tap on the back arrow/Cancel.

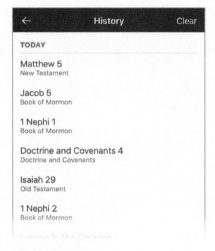

OVERLAPPING SQUARES

I am not sure what the overlapping square icon is for. I tap on it, and a screen list appears. It may only have one item or many. I tap on Edit and see the same type of setup as in the bookmarks edit list. I am not exactly sure what the purpose is, but I am pretty sure it will not help me to add content to my collection. However, I want to come back to this later to see what it does. I tap on Done and then Cancel.

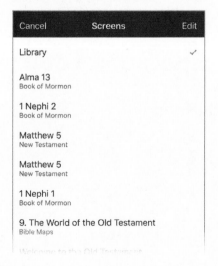

SEARCH

I am pretty sure that the magnifying glass icon is for searches. I know because I have seen it used in many different applications and it is always for searching.

I tap on it, and a search window opens and perhaps a list of past searches. I decide that is not going to move content into my collection. I also want to come back to this feature to see exactly how it works. I tap on Done.

SETTINGS

In the lower left-hand corner, I see a gear icon. I tap on it and see that it contains various setting options. I scroll down to see if there might be a collection setting, but I do not find anything. However, I have learned where to find the settings, so I make a mental note.

Using UI, I want to know how to get out of Settings. Starting in the upper left-hand corner and going across, I see Done. I tap on that and find myself back at the Library.

At this point I am starting to get discouraged, but I have one last area to check, and that is the middle of the screen. I tap on my personal collection "Gospel Doctrine Class." I scan the screen, starting in the upper left-hand corner, and see nothing that would allow me to add something to the collection.

I then think maybe I need to go to another collection, and from there I can add to my personal collection. Since I am building content for my Gospel Doctrine class in the Library, I tap on Lessons. I once again move clockwise around the screen, and the only thing I see that might help is Edit. I tap on Edit.

This looks familiar. I scan the screen and see at the bottom is Add to . . ., but it is ghosted. I tap on Sunday School and see options for Remove and Download, but Add to . . . is still ghosted.

I tap on Sunday School again to remove the check mark and tap on Done. I then tap on Sunday School and see the Old Testament: Gospel Doctrine manual.

With a quick scan, I see Edit and tap on that. I am now getting used to seeing these empty circles and know what to do. I tap on *Old Testament: Gospel Doctrine*, and a check mark appears. I scan the screen and see that Add to . . . is available.

I tap on Add to . . ., and there I can see my new Gospel Doctrine Class collection.

I scan the screen and see the plus sign. I tap on it because that would be the most logical choice. Instead it apparently allows me to create a new custom collection. I have learned that I can create a custom collection on the fly. I scan the screen and tap on Cancel.

The only choice left is to tap on Gospel Doctrine Class. I tap on it, and a message in a blue band notifies me the content has been added to the Gospel Doctrine Class.

Note: I could have also tried touching and holding on *Old Testament: Gospel Doctrine* and would have found that an option to Add to . . . was also available.

OBSERVATION

The above exercise appears to take a considerable amount of time, but it really only takes a few seconds. This is the technique that the tech-savvy use, and you can learn to do it also. Like all things, practice is required, and the key is simply developing the habit of scanning the screen and interacting with what you see.

PRINCIPLE REVIEW

Notice that I always started in the upper left-hand corner and worked clockwise, and I am fearless in tapping an icon to see what lies beneath it.

The process is simple—observe, interact, assess, and then repeat if needed.

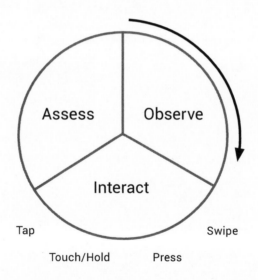

WHEN UI AWARENESS IS NOT ENOUGH

Sometimes UI awareness is not enough. A function is not always located in a logical place—for example, history in the bookmark list in the iPhone. When UI fails, we have to turn to other resources.

For the Gospel Library, one resource is the Tips collection in the Gospel Library found at the very end of the Collections.

If Tips does not answer your questions, you can email me at help@thebusylatterdaysaint.com, and I will answer your question. Also, there is always your friend—Google.

The last resort to getting an answer is sending an email to the developer of the application. Developers want people to continue using their application and want to get good reviews, so they are generally responsive to questions and suggestions. Contact information can be found in settings or the help section. If not, then check their website.

The Gospel Library makes it very easy to ask for help or offer suggestions for improvement.

For iOS, go to Settings / Send Feedback.

For Android, go to the option menu / Settings / Send Feedback.

PERSONAL PHILOSOPHY

Before leaving the subject of being UI aware, I share with you my personal philosophy of working with applications.

If I download an application and within a fairly short period of time cannot figure out how use it, I delete it. If an app is not user friendly, I am not interested in using it. The purpose of an application is to make my life easier, not more difficult.

Of course, there are exceptions to this rule. If an app has received great reviews and is very popular, or I see that the app could be of great value to me, such as the Gospel Library, then I am willing to take longer—a few days or even a few weeks—to learn how to use it. Most likely I will find the manual by searching Google for it and then can quickly peruse it. A quick perusal will generally answer about 90 percent of my questions. The other 10 percent I will search Google to find the answer or write the developer.

There have been times that I have downloaded a popular app and, while I found it interesting, I did not see the value of making it a part of my life: Evernote is a great example.

I downloaded Evernote when it first came out, played around with it, and didn't see what the big deal was, so I deleted it. Then about two years later, I read an article about how the author was using Evernote, and the proverbial light came on. I downloaded the app and have been using it ever since.

Also, there is no such thing as a perfect application. Every app has inconsistencies, flaws, quirkiness, and, at times, bugs. I do not look for perfection, though I hope for it. Despite the imperfections, if the application makes my life easier or helps me to fulfill my responsibilities, then I am willing to work with it.

CONCLUSION

It has been quite a journey. I hope that you have enjoyed it.

The Lord has blessed us with technology and applications such as the Gospel Library so that we can delve into the scriptures in ways that were not previously possible. He has provided a way that we can have scriptures, conference talks, manuals, videos, and other material in our hands so that we can make the best use of our time.

We have been blessed with devices that—through music and the spoken word—can help keep us on the straight and narrow as we listen occasionally during the day and when feeling down.

We are in the last days, and we need to help in hastening His work. We have a tremendous responsibility in doing so, and that device that you hold in your hands is one of the keys to fulfilling your responsibilities.

Within your hands is the power to spread the gospel throughout the world, to bear testimony, to send a message that lifts another, to make better use of your time, and to more effectively study the scriptures and teach.

I hope that you have developed the habit of studying the scriptures daily and found joy and spiritual growth in doing so.

I now ask that you take what you have learned and teach others; become a Gospel Library missionary. Bear your testimony, when appropriate, about the strength, power, and growth that come from daily scripture study, and teach others about the Gospel Library.

When you sit next to someone and see there is something you can teach them about using the Gospel Library, find a time to share with them just one idea, and watch their face light up.

We truly live in a marvelous age; how blessed we are to be part of this great work.

ABOUT THE AUTHOR

Richard Bernard is an experienced teacher, speaker, and unabashed technology geek. Because of his dyslexia, Richard has struggled his entire life finding how to manage his time and to study and understand the scriptures. He found the answer in technology and came to see that what he learned is applicable to everyone. He loves technology and has been teaching its use since the mid '80s. He served a two-year service mission at the Missionary Training Center in Provo, Utah, helping missionaries effectively study the scriptures. As tablets were introduced at the MTC, he helped in developing lessons incorporating the Gospel Library in their scripture study. He is passionate about the Gospel Library and has been a guest speaker in California and Utah and a teacher at BYU Education Week.

For further help and videos,
scan to visit

TheBusyLatterDaySaint.com